For Diane

With sincere appreciation and
many fond memories from
"the Class of 89."

1st

Steve
Smith

Anne
Moody

Pam Wilkinson

Cathie Winters

Judith
Miller

MATTHEW
KUHASZ

Trasi
McCart

NOT QUITE
A HORSEWOMAN

NOT QUITE
A HORSEWOMAN

Caroline Akrill

ILLUSTRATED BY ANNE PILGRIM
FOREWORD BY DORIAN WILLIAMS, OBE

ALLEN

NOT QUITE A HORSEWOMAN
first published October 1982 by
Arlington Books (Publishers) Ltd
15–17 King Street
St James's London SW1

Reprinted July 1983
First published in this
paperback edition 1988

© Caroline Akrill 1982
© Illustrations Anne Pilgrim 1982

Set in England by
Inforum Ltd Portsmouth
Printed and bound in England by
Billing & Sons Ltd
Worcester and London

British Library Cataloguing in Publication Data
Akrill, Caroline
Not quite a horsewoman
1. Horsemanship — Personal observations
I. Title
798.2'092'4
ISBN 0-05140-727-7

To my husband
and not-so-small daughter
with love

CONTENTS

One way and another there is a good deal of Red Tape at the Meet; much of it is actually tied onto the horses' tails . . . It is a good thing to tie tape on to *all* the dangerous points of your horse and then no one can say they weren't warned. You could also tie warnings *on to yourself* . . . . reading HOPELESSLY STUPID or QUITE OUT OF CONTROL, or even NOT QUITE A G*NTL*M*N, so that people will know what to do about you.

From *Horse Nonsense* by Yeatman and Sellar, published by Methuen London.

Foreword

It has always seemed to me that far too many people who ride, breed horses or ponies, show, hunt – or, in fact, are involved with horses in any way – tend to take it all much too seriously.

Surely, if anything should be fun it is riding. It costs one dearly; it takes up a great deal of time and, all too often it ends in disappointment, frustration, sometimes even disaster. At the very least one should enjoy it.

Equally, it is true that most books on any aspect of equestrianism – and there are certainly enough of them – are rather serious efforts; the authors tending to take themselves even more seriously than those for whom they are writing.

From all that is written in *Not Quite a Horsewoman*, it is quite obvious that Caroline Akrill can never be accused of having taken her riding too seriously. More important, she does not take her writing too seriously either.

In fact, this book, a collection of some of the best articles that she has contributed to various horsy magazines, is sometimes hilarious, always very amusing: made the more so by the fact that it is obvious that Caroline Akrill is very knowledgeable about the serious side of what she writes about in a far from serious vein.

Reading these articles one realises that there is something autobiographical in the experiences she describes so amusingly. Perhaps it is that she identifies herself so accurately with the hundreds of 'riding mothers' who go through it all with first ponies, long-suffering husbands, deceptive advertisements and all the aggravations connected with showing or hunting, or riding schools, or driving, or the Pony Club.

The great thing is to be able to laugh at oneself – and this is most certainly what Caroline Akrill can do. Recently reviewing her novel, *Eventer's Dream*, I remarked on her witty, brilliant characterisations which, in fact, I suggested stood comparison with some of those by Somerville and Ross in *Memoirs of an Irish R.M.* This book confirms that she very really has the gift of the humorous writer.

There are plenty of authors who can tackle the equestrian field seriously. It is far more difficult to tackle it amusingly. This is why everyone reading this book will get from it immense enjoyment.

Dorian Williams.

Introducing Mrs Akrill

The over-riding impression one may be left with after perusing this anthology is that my labours in the pursuit of the Art of Horse(wo)manship have been a dismal failure, a catalogue of ineptitude wherein not a day has dawned, not a task been attempted, that did not end in anguish.

This is almost true. Yet, here and there, perhaps only between the lines, it may be possible to glimpse the fleeting moment of absolute joy, the inconstant pleasure, the miniature triumph, that brings people like me, trapped by a terrible fascination for the horse world and the perils that lurk within, and even after the most crushing of humiliations, creeping inexorably back for yet another try.

In the course of my horsy experiences I have tried (and it has to be said, failed) most things; not only was I once the proprietor of the worst riding school in the world, but ran for a while what was quite possibly the most unsuccessful show pony stable ever. I have attempted to master the Art of Riding to Hounds, and I have also been a horse dealer of sorts, both of the latter whilst helping to run a country pub which suffered dreadfully from my divided interests.

My writing career is, at the time of publication, scarcely more than ten years old; it only seems like a lifetime. *The Retirement of Mrs Akrill* was the first thing I ever wrote and it was published by Elwyn Hartley Edwards, then editor of *Riding* magazine. Other articles followed and I was promoted to roving reporter covering shows and visiting studs with varying degrees of success.

It must be admitted that not everyone enjoyed what I wrote.

"I have had cause to complain about your reporting before," one show president wrote, "but your last effort is more than any of us can stand, and I have asked the editor not to send you to any of our future shows."

One commission that still sticks in the gullet was the time I was dispatched to Tidworth Horse Trials in lieu of one whose knowledge of such things was considerably greater than mine. This was a new and frightening experience. I sat stolidly through hundreds of dressage tests, stood for hours on end on the baked and dusty steeplechase course, trailed endlessly round the cross-country fences, gave myself neck-ache staring hopelessly up at score boards, the calculations of which defeated me utterly. Afterwards I toiled and struggled over my copy late into the night to the vast amusement of experienced professionals like Leslie Lane and Cynthia Muir, the former who managed without any apparent effort on his part, to be in exactly the right place at the right time, and the latter who, laced with dogs of amazing variety, never within my sight wrote down a word.

When the article subsequently appeared in *Riding* as *Tidworth in Pictures*, together with a terse list of placings and minus every word of my sweated copy, it was regarded as the joke of the century and it took a long time to shake off the title *Our Special Eventing Correspondent*. How surprising then, that Arlington Books should ask me to write an eventing trilogy although, as one of their directors pointed out after reading the rough copy for this introduction, had they known about the Tidworth incident, they might have had second thoughts.

The trilogy of novels must go down on record as one of my successes but one must also add that it is not yet finished. *Eventer's Dream* and *A Hoof in the Door* are in the bag, but when it comes to writing the third and last book, *Ticket to Ride*, set in the world of top eventing, I may have to leave the country.

It was entirely due to publicity surrounding the publication of *Eventer's Dream* that I got the chance to become a regular broadcaster on Radio Orwell as the resident horse and pony expert on a Sunday morning children's programme called *Boomerang*. I am not a natural comedian and all the advice and information I have to offer on the radio is delivered in a solemn manner and from comprehensive notes which are a source of wonder and amusement to the presenters of the programme. I have become used to it now, but at first the sudden insertion of a noisy record during a lecture on external parasites of the horse, or the interruption, as I explain how to assess the age of a pony by its teeth, with a shouted, "What do you give a horse with a cough?" followed by the response, "Cough Stirrup!" together with a burst of laughter, throws me into a confusion from which even my carefully prepared notes cannot save me.

After a few months of broadcasting from the studio it was decided that we should add authenticity to the programme by taking ourselves and our recording equipment to a local stable yard where, to a background of clopping hooves and the scrape of pitchforks, we delivered advice on basic stable management. On the morning of the broadcast I sat at home and listened. What I heard were a lot of scraping noises, a few disjointed sentences, and a high-pitched whine followed by a small explosion. It was all not quite how I had imagined it and shortly afterwards I was given away to another radio station.

Pony magazine has been one of the loves of my life, and Michael Williams, ex-editor of both *Pony* and *Light Horse*, never failed to encourage his contributors, ever spurring them to greater efforts and thus proving that they could write, when the rest of the world and even they themselves doubted it. It was for *Light Horse* that I ventured back into the hunting field after an absence of fifteen years, at great risk to personal safety and financial stability. It is an experience I look back upon with enjoyment and affection, but with absolutely no desire to repeat.

When *Light Horse* went up in a puff of smoke only to reappear in the same instant as the revamped *Horse and Rider*, I was both surprised and gratified to be recalled to the ranks as a regular columnist.

In my time I had been many things, but a columnist never. When I told my family what I had become, they shrugged their shoulders and professed themselves unsurprised. It was only later I discovered they thought I had said communist. Their calm acceptance was slightly unnerving in the light of the fact that I have always considered myself a true blue. But enough of politics.

Let me not fail in this introduction to offer my most grateful thanks to those magazines which have given immediate and unstinting permission for articles which first appeared amongst their pages to be reproduced in this anthology, and with which I have been honoured to enjoy the happiest (and by the way this is going, the most sycophantic and toadying) of relationships: *Riding, Horse and Rider, Pony, Light Horse, Hoofprint, Horse and Pony,* and last, but certainly not least of all, *The Field*.

So here you have it: an autobiographical anthology comprising the exploits and reflections of an incompetent horsewoman, bungling reporter, unsuccessful show pony producer, disgraceful riding school proprietor, reluctant foxhunter and exploding broadcaster; proof, even in these hard times when we must tighten our girths as well as our belts in order to survive, that it is still perfectly possible to make a career out of misadventure and ineptitude.

Caroline Akrill
Suffolk 1982

Success is often born of the most unpromising situations. In 1982 my editor at Arlington Books, Christine Lunness, gazed at me over a vast pile of yellowing magazine clippings and said, 'Caroline, we are *never* going to make a book out of this.' But we did, and here it is, resplendent in its third edition, reprinted and represented by (so they tell me) Popular Demand.

I was once reinstated as a columnist by Popular Demand in a magazine which, anxious to make amends, announced CAROLINE'S BACK! in large, ego-flattering letters on their cover. Publication was swiftly followed by an indignant letter accusing them of misrepresentation which began, 'Being a back sufferer myself, I was encouraged to buy your magazine on the strength of the cover of your February issue . . .'

It *is* nice to be back.

THE ART OF
HORSE(WO)MANSHIP

Urgent Message to all Novice Riders. GET OUT WHILST THERE IS STILL TIME. The whole thing, I tell you, is one enormous conspiracy. There is no such thing as the Art of Horse(wo)manship.

Most people believe that the Art of Horse(wo)manship was invented by the Ancient Greeks. This is not so. It is a devilish scheme jointly devised by the British Horse Society and the Association of British Riding Schools in order to relieve us of our last pound note in pursuit of the impossible dream – that of becoming the Compleat Horse(wo)man.

I can reveal to you here and now, that you haven't a hope of becoming the Compleat Horse(wo)man at all; you are more likely to fly unaided first. The reason for this is simple. It is because the first principle of the scheme is to make sure you stay a novice for the rest of your life; they wait until you are within an eyelash of becoming proficient, and then they change the rules. Thus, once you are on the treadmill, you will spend a lifetime learning and unlearning, learning and unlearning, and having the teachings of one instructor (because they never quite agree upon the Finer Points of the Art of Horse(wo)manship, this being an essential part of the plot), corrected by the next.

My friend Elaine, having endured thirty years of instruction, yet knowing herself to be the Incompleat Horse(wo)man, recently signed on with yet another top instructor for an assessment lesson. The result of this assessment, after half an hour of agonising contortions performed upon an equine robot at the end of a lunge, was, 'Shows Potential'.

"Is it possible," Elaine wondered, "to 'show potential' at thirty-six years of age? Or is it time to throw in the cap?"

Consider, if you will, my own position. Almost certainly, I must rate as one of the most tutored riders in the land; there is hardly an instructor alive who has not had a hand in my seat at one time or another. Yet here I am, having parted with half a fortune and approaching forty years of age; baffled, bewildered, incompetent, and just as far from being the Compleat Horse(wo)man as ever. Is it any wonder that when I think of all those beginner riders wobbling unsteadily towards a similar fate, I could weep?

But there is worse to come, because when you finally abandon all hope of becoming the Compleat Horse(wo)man, and hang up your boots for good, you will be faced with yet another appalling discovery. You can't get rid of your redundant equines. They are *Passengers for Life*.

You can't sell redundant equines because nobody answers your advertisements. The only people who do reply are those who make a career out of selling their own equines through other people's advertisements. If you sell yours, they say, would you be *oh so kind* and pass on any surplus enquiries as, *strange as it may seem*, your advertisement describes our horses exactly.

You can't give away redundant equines either, because the people you decide to give them to have already decided to give you theirs. And you can forget about packing them off to a sale, because unless you have a heart of stone, the thought of them being shipped On the Hoof will cause the hairs to rise on the back of your neck. No, you are stuck with them. It is a *Life Sentence*.

Moreover, redundant equines have a habit of becoming old; and old redundant equines need more of everything. More attention. More veterinary care. More warm blankets. More food. So you trundle up and down with rugs and bales of hay, and you double-glaze the stable, and you bulk-buy vast quantities of oats and bran and flaked maize and milk pellets, and you soak beet pulp in the bath, and you lose your wellingtons in the gateways and you fish dead birds out of the trough, and you wish with all your heart that you had never heard of the Art of Horse(wo)manship.

The team of workmen I engaged to erect an escape-proof post and rail fence around my redundant equines professed themselves curious because they never saw me ride. Did I, they enquired, construct obstacles with the coloured poles and wings and fly over them television-style? No, I said. Not any more. These days they were just kept for decoration; they were a status symbol. But what about the horses, they wanted to know. Did I ride the bridle paths, or harness them to the cart with yellow wheels, glimpsed amongst the trees of the orchard? No, I said. They were pets. These days I preferred to look at them over the fence. Once a horse-owner, I told them, always a horse owner. Naturally, they didn't understand. They went away totally mystified, leaving me with a bill for an amount only marginally less than the cost of the land their fence surrounded.

The Art of Horse(wo)manship has the devil of a lot to answer for.

There is Safety in Numnahs

At the Martini Awards, the managing director of D.J. Murphy Limited presented me to a gentleman who, with his first breath and almost before the introduction was over, quite openly and loudly declared that he loathed and detested horses.

Not one whit disturbed by this outrageous and, considering the company, even slightly dangerous statement, the managing director continued smoothly upon her introductory path. "Then you two should get on very well together," she said firmly, "because Caroline can't stand them either."

This is not exactly true. I love horses. To me they are fascinating, lovable and delightful creatures; useful, affectionate, intelligent, graceful, and extremely beautiful to look at. On the other hand, many years of familiarity has shown me that they are also infuriatingly stupid, incomprehensible beasts; dirty, unfriendly, ugly, ungrateful, expensive and horribly dangerous.

Do not imagine though, that I am alone in feeling like this, because a love/hate relationship has been going on between woman and horse ever since the first equine tip-toed out of the forest on its four-pronged hoof to be speared and roasted by the first horse-lover. This love/hate relationship is vividly chronicled in the plethora of Olde Englishe Sayings and Proverbs which have been faithfully handed down to us from horsy generation to generation. For example, "He that fights and runs away, may live to fry another grey." Or, as evidence that an unrelenting diet of Equus Robustus could become monotonous, "Tomorrow is another bay," and proving that the beast was no less obliging in the stone age than he is now, "You can catch my black, and I'll catch yours."

Apart from the old horse chestnuts such as, "Never cook a gift horse in the Aga," and, "If wishes were horses, beggars would be better fed," there are many more time-honoured expressions in every-day use whose meaning is not so glaringly obvious. Thus, although the golden rule of driving, "Never put the cart before the horse," is unnecessarily explicit, because any fool knows it fits behind, it is perhaps not quite so well known that the familiar proverb, "Many hands make light work," means the bigger the horse, the more work it can be expected to do.

The breeders' maxim, "Foals and their mummies are soon parted," needs no explanation, but it may not be well known that the first saddle was invented by the person who discovered the truth of, "Ride comes before a fall." The problems involved in making the saddle fit were responsible for the phrase, "There is safety in numnahs," whilst Epsom Salts were first prescribed for horses after a prolonged and agonising case of equine constipation, when for three weeks there was found to be, "Nothing new under the dun." More cheering news though, for those beset with stable vices, for although, "Too many crib-biters spoil the trough," it is certainly true to say that "One swallow does not make a windsucker."

Keeping horses in the manner to which we have become accustomed is a costly business, and with the horse clearly in mind, "Two is company, three is too expensive," was coined; and the appalling cost of corn and best quality hay was probably foremost in the thoughts of the person who first muttered, "As one jaw closes, another jaw opens."

Dressage and eventing are fairly recent sports, but high school and manege riding have ancient origins; thus, "Piaffe and the world piaffes with you," is a much older proverb than, "You can ride a horse to water but you cannot make it jump," which precedes, "It is easy to be wise after the Three-Day Event," by only a few minutes.

The unfortunate rider who has discovered that, "He who hesitates is tossed," will probably run home at once to fulfil the old adage, "Always lock the stable door after the horse has bolted," realising that there is a sporting chance that the brute will try to come back. It is as well to bear in mind though, that there is nothing in the world so unbearably nostalgic to a horsewoman as an empty stable. "They are not long, the days of equine and horses."

Ah, "Those were the greys . . ."

Legs Like Nutcrackers

Riding School Pupils everywhere, regardless of age, ability and sex, PAY ATTENTION. The following information could Change Your Life. You are about to learn something, as they say in legal circles, To Your Advantage.

In the course of my research, which has spanned almost four decades and involved more riding schools than you would believe, I have made important discoveries. One of the most glaringly obvious discoveries is that the riding school horse has evolved into a specific type with palpable characteristics common to the species. One of these characteristics is not going into the corners.

Now as any riding school habitué knows, not going into the corners is a Mortal Sin, probably tantamount to murder, certainly worse than adultery, and yet no weekly pupil (or even twice-weekly pupil) can produce the effortlessly supple curvature of the riding school horse's spine necessary for this simple exercise, because try as you and I might, the brute sets his mouth like a plank, and almost before we have realised it, he has cut smartly across the corner with as much curve in his spinal column as there is in a broom handle.

The reason for this is simple, and it is directly related to another significant characteristic of the riding school horse, which is an extremely refined sensibility that informs the brute, even as you lift your foot to the stirrup (thus enabling it to move fractionally out of range), that you are not a person of authority in the saddle.

Surprisingly, being a person of authority in the saddle has nothing at all to do with the things you might expect, like having a commanding grip on the reins, a bullying manner, or a big smacker on the end of your whip, because none of these things cut any ice with the riding school horse whatsoever. I can now reveal that when the instructor tells you wearily to dismount in order that he or she can take to the saddle and display Authoritarian Horse(wo)manship, making the riding school horse curl round the corners like a bendy toy and making you and I look absolute fools in front of the rest of the class, what he or she has got that you and I haven't are *legs like nutcrackers*.

Believe me when I tell you that legs like nutcrackers are not achieved in five minutes. They are the end result of riding for six hours a day, six days a week, for six months, and preferably for six years. It can be deduced from this then, that you and I, riding for a mere hour or two per week, have absolutely no chance of being mistaken for a person of authority in the saddle at all. But take heart. My carefully devised exercise routine has been expressly designed to gradually develop muscles you don't even know you have, giving you legs like iron bands, capable of squeezing the evasions and the breath out of any riding school horse in the land.

Exercise 1. Place an orange (or similar sized circular object, but preferably not an egg) about 30cm away from your feet. With your hands clasped to your elbows behind your back (for the improvement of posture), pick up the orange with your knees, stand upright, then replace the orange. Repeat 20 times.

Exercise 2. Walk upstairs with your knees pressed tightly together, clasping the elbows behind your back as before. Coming down is easier but of doubtful benefit.

. . . the ideal time to perfect the low growl

Exercise 3. Place three books between your knees (these should be octavo size for your own comfort) and go for a walk. If the middle one falls out, you are not doing the exercise properly. Work up to half a mile daily.

The above exercise routine, if followed faithfully for one month, will promote a vice-like pincer action of the legs which might transform you into a person of authority in the saddle, although you may first prefer to read the warning letter which follows later.

Another basic characteristic of the riding school horse, discovered during my research, is blatant unresponsiveness. Blatant unresponsiveness is the prime cause of numbing fatigue in the riding school pupil who is forced to flail arms and legs and even jump up and down in the saddle to produce any semblance of movement at all. The truth is that blatantly unresponsive riding school horses only ever come to life when the instructor swings into the saddle in order to demonstrate to the rest of the class that it isn't actually the horse that is at fault, but the rider. Naturally, as soon as the riding school pupil regains the saddle, the beast is as blatantly unresponsive as ever.

The secret of success with blatantly unresponsive riding school horses is the *low growl*. The low growl never fails, and it has the advantage to both woman and beast that you only have to apply the ash plant once. At the first sign of blatant unresponsiveness, the riding school pupil must emit a low, threatening growl from the back of the throat which increases rapidly in volume, together with the lightning application of the ash plant on both sides of the ribs. This never fails to provoke instant and horrified acceleration in even the most hardened blatantly unresponsive riding school horse, being reminiscent to the equine mind of primitive unseen terrors such as tigers in trees and the like. Thereupon, the flailing of arms and legs and the futile bouncing of the buttocks on the saddle, and the thwackings with the ash plant will be totally redundant; the low growl itself will be sufficient. It works like a charm.

Practice is necessary, however, to produce a low growl with enough resonance and the right amount of menace. The ideal time to perfect the low growl is when you are practising the nutcracker exercises, perhaps when walking briskly along a quiet lane with three books between your knees. It could change your life.

When this article first appeared in *Horse and Rider* it provoked the following response from a reader.

> *The Editor,*
> *Horse and Rider.*
> *Madam,*
>   *Caroline Akrill looks and sounds charming, humorous and pathetic. Her amusing article in your August issue describes the plight and frustrations of the week-end rider on the riding school horse so vividly and sympathetically that it must reflect personal experience. However, she ought to be told, and her readers warned, to give up her recipe for disaster as soon as possible.*
>   *She must surely have heard at some time that one of the most desirable attributes of a rider is a flat inner thigh. She is, I fear, busy developing instead a cylinder of cast iron, which may take months of rest in bed and daily massage to reduce to serviceable proportions. All time need not be*

wasted, because she can continue to practice the low growl. It isn't mentioned as an aid in classical text books, perhaps because it would be penalised in dressage tests.

Nicole Bartle,
The Yorkshire Riding Centre.

A lot depends, of course, on whether or not one could actually live with a flat inner thigh. Is it a noticeable deformity? What will it look like on the beach? Together with the hacking cough, the horseman's ear, and the horsemaid's knee, will it ultimately prove too big a price to pay for the Art of Horse(wo)manship?

* * *

When I first wrote the next piece it was returned to me by the editorial department of *Horse and Rider* as unsuitable for publication, with the following verses:

> Ode to a Broken ***T
>
> Dear Caroline, we feel
> An explanation must be due
> As to why we are returning
> This manuscript to you.
>
> The staff at *Horse and Rider*
> Cannot be labelled prude,
> In fact it makes a change to read
> An article that's rude!
> But as publishers we feel
> We must protect the public mind
> We fear it might disturb
> To read a story of this kind.
>
> Our jobs would be in grave dispute,
> Nothing left for it but the boot!
> And spare a thought for our MD,

Who would no doubt blush to see
This P/A speciality!

So, regretfully we return
The erring manuscript post haste,
And look forward to receiving
Another in its place.

The article is printed here as I first wrote it. However, *Horse and Rider* did eventually publish it with the ****ing bits removed and, amazingly, as you will see, it inspired yet more verse.

*Oink, Oink, ****!*

Could there be, amongst our readers, some truly knowledgeable person who is able to solve the problem of the oink? Many people think that only pigs oink, but in my youth I had a piebald pony who oinked all the time. Being as sensitive then as I am now, I was greatly embarrassed by the oinks, as in the well-known verse, ". . . the rumblings abdominal were simply phenomenal," I was terribly afraid that people would think it was me.

The mysterious oink didn't happen at the walk, or at the canter, or even at the gallop; it happened at the trot. I tried very hard to minimise the effect by varying the speed of the pace, but it was to no avail. Trotting along slower made the oinks, though relatively spaced out, more noticeable than ever; and a faster trot increased the volume and frequency to alarming proportions, producing a noise not unlike the mating call of the hump-backed whale. Eventually I only ever trotted the piebald pony in the privacy of his own paddock and never ever down the village street, where there were people to stare in curiosity and reproach as we oinked past. It was all very inconvenient.

Whenever I met a knowledgeable horsy person, I demanded to

know where the distressing oinks originated from. The first know-ledgeable horsy person declared it to be wind under the saddle. When I informed my family that the piebald pony was suffering from wind under the saddle, it caused great alarm and despondency. If it was indeed wind under the saddle, they cried, then how could it possibly be avoided, when all the textbooks insisted upon a gap betwixt saddle and spine where any amount of wind could collect, presumably to be oinked out at the first opportunity? They made haste to exchange the saddle for a flatter, dangerously close-fitting model. The oinking continued.

The second knowledgeable horsy person informed me that the oinking was due to dyspepsia; the piebald's diet was at fault. We tried everything. We soaked sugar beet pulp, chopped chaff, boiled barley, sliced roots, damped his feeds more, gave him his food dry. Finally, as a last-ditch effort, we put Epsom Salts in his water. The result of this was lamentable and dyed his hocks orange, but it didn't stop the oinking.

The third knowledgeable horsy person announced that the cause of the oinking was air being bounced out of the lungs by bad riding. I had no idea that the piebald pony had lungs under the saddle, but my family, having no false illusions about my riding ability, were convinced that this must be true. Better riders than I were placed upon the piebald's unnecessarily new saddle; I was not entirely displeased when the oinking continued.

In a final gesture of defeat, the oinking piebald was sold and an improved, silent-running model took its place. The saddle didn't fit. The family took it back to the saddlers who exchanged it for the original, charging them a mere twenty pounds for the privilege of ending up with the saddle they had owned in the first place.

Worse, oh far, far worse though, than the piebald pony's oink, was the little bay cob's ****. My little bay cob ****ed quite a lot. I didn't like it. Once more, knowledgeable horsy people were inclined to blame it on his diet. Once more I tried everything. Nothing worked; he still ****ed. When I was riding out in company, I kept a covert eye on other people's horses. They didn't seem to **** at all. It didn't seem exactly fair.

The little bay cob had two distinct types of ****. Any sudden burst of violent activity, such as being set free in the paddock, or hurtling into a gallop after the "Gone Away", would precipitate a rapid succession of exceedingly loud and shocking ****s which would cause everyone within firing distance to fall backwards in confusion, scanning the landscape for trombone players, artillery or crow-scarers. I was gone, of course, before they fully understood what had happened.

Rather worse than this was the stationary ****. This would invariably occur at some smart Riding Club function, or at a lawn meet when I was engaged in genteel conversation with friends on their non-****ing equines. The stationary **** would begin inno-cently and softly enough, slowly and inevitably rising to a deafening crescendo which was most distressingly prolonged and almost impossible to ignore. I was forced to sell the little bay cob in the end. He only ****ed once when the new purchasers came to try him as he took off over an upright fence. I waited for them to say, "Does he do that often?" but they appeared not to notice.

The cause of the oink remains a mystery, but the problem of the **** is not new. In the latter part of the eighteenth century, a troubled gentleman referred his problem to the infamous Geoffrey Gambado, Master of Horse to the Doge of Venice, who in turn, referred it to his farrier. His reply, which subsequently appeared in the learned work, *Annals of Horsemanship*, was as follows:

Honoured Sir,
By advice from Mr Gambado of your horse's complaint, I have sent you a powder so strong, that if administer'd night and morning in his corn, will be bold to say no horse in England shall ever fart again after Thursday next. Shall be very thankful for your Honour's custom in the same way in future, and your lady's too, if agreeable; being, Honoured Sir,
Your Servant to Command, Jo. Wood.

I might still have been riding the little bay cob if he had appended the recipe.

* * *

When the revised version of this article appeared in the magazine I received the following advice from two readers.

> The Editor
> Horse & Rider.
>
> Madam,
> I've often heard the Oinkings
> Of which you columnise,
> "Where does it emanate from?"
> I hear your plaintive cries:
>
> It's air trapped near his thingy
> That dangles underneath,
> And when a gelding's slightly tense,
> It Oinks out, from his sheath!
>
> > Well informed,
> > Scarborough.
>
> Dear Caroline,
> In answer to your pitiful cry:
> "My horse goes 'Oink', please tell me why."
> I would agree, a pig he's not,
> Although he 'Oinks' when at the trot.
>
> If he is a gelding piebald,
> Emitting 'Oinks' so very ribald,
> I would suggest that, every other week
> With soap and water you clean his sheath;
> This will stop his 'Oinking' crib,
> And make him feel less like a pig!
>
> > D. Jarvis.
> > (ex King's Troop Royal Horse Artillery)

Anything But A Groom

Desperation and a distinct lack of enthusiastic response to the advertised post of part-time groom at seven shillings and sixpence an hour, brought me Rita. Lately promoted from spasmodic contributor to the exalted position of hunting correspondent and having two hunters, a mare and her unweaned foal, a pony livery and an unbroken three-year-old filly to cope with, I was ready and eager to become an employer when I engaged this solitary applicant over the telephone. But Rita, when she arrived, looked anything but a groom.

. . . she nearly frightened the master to death

She was fortyish and highly strung and built like a beanpole, with a long, thin, pancaked face, lividly rouged cheeks and round, anxious eyes, topped by the most amazing eyebrows, which appeared to have been drawn with orange crayon using a penny as a template. The orange crayon matched Rita's hair exactly. It was cut short and stood upright without any visible means of support, like a burning bush or an early punk, except that punks hadn't been invented in 1974. When, on the occasion of a tarmac meet on the pub car park, the master of the Puckeridge and Thurlow Hunt first clapped eyes on Rita, she nearly frightened him to death. "Good God!" he bellowed. "What's that?"

"That's the landlady's new groom, sir," the terrier-man informed him solemnly.

The family found Rita's appointment as groom hysterical. It was quite impossible for anyone even to mention her name without invoking a lot of unseemly mirth and it wasn't all directed at Rita; a lot was directed at me. As far as I was concerned, I could feel in my bones that I was about to be exploited again. I was no stranger to exploitation. After suffering blatant exploitation in my early career as a trainee and an employee, it might have been reasonable to suppose that when the tables turned and I found myself in the position of employer, I might have been well placed to get my own back. Not so. Towards the end of my riding school days I woke up one morning and realised that I had become a slave to my own working pupils. Far from the usual cry of working pupils being used as unpaid servants, the unpaid servant was me.

I taught my pupils, cooked for them, cleaned their untidy rooms, washed their unspeakably filthy clothes, arbitrated in their silly disagreements, nursed them when they were sick, acted as their chauffeur, housekeeper, general factotum and Guru. When, ahead of my time, I introduced the five-day week, they refused to go home on their days off. Finally, I was forced to close the school in order to get rid of them and on the last day we all wept tears of genuine regret. Not one of them, as far as I know, ever passed their exams.

The saddest thing about Rita was that she desperately needed the money, pathetic amount that it was. On the morning she started work she had confided to me that her husband was in prison and right away the tears spilled out of the round, anxious eyes, furrowing through the pancake and the rouge; it was all very upsetting. She had turned up dressed in a collection of mis-shapen cardigans of various hues, a pair of hideously loud brown and orange check trousers, and the only pair of shoes she had in the world. I sent her off to the saddlery with a ten pound note with which to fit herself out with a pair of rubber riding boots, because I could see that the only pair of shoes she had in the world weren't going to last five minutes in my yard. Sartorially, at least, this proved to be a mistake, because anxious to display all she could of the shiny new boots, she cobbled the brown and orange check trousers into breeches, and looked more like Coco the Clown than ever.

All this might have been endured, but as a groom Rita was hopeless. She just hadn't a clue. Mucking out one stable took her all morning and at the end of it all there would be more clean straw on the muck heap than in the stable. She found the water buckets too heavy, so she only half filled them, and she misread the feedchart, stuffing the nursing mother with corn so that she became unusually hot to handle, whilst the hunters, bursting at their seams with bulk foods and milk supplements, laboured in the wake of the field, puffing like a pair of grampuses, never getting a glimpse of hounds, other than at the meet, for the rest of the season.

Rita was useless as a strapper, fiddling about with the sort of uncertain, nervous strokes that turn the most docile animal into a fidget, and she could strip a bridle for cleaning and put it together like a Rubik's Cube. Even I, who had in my youth won a hoof pick for reassembling a double bridle in record time, was almost defeated.

But if Rita was terrible in the stables with the horses, she was far, far worse on top of them. She rode like a water-skier, with her hands under her chin, her feet stuck stiffly forward, and her eyes rolling round and round in apparent terror, although she swore that she enjoyed it. After a few chance meetings with my smart horsy neighbours in the lanes, Rita was confined to the yard.

It was a rare week that Rita had any money to draw on pay day, because she always needed to borrow it in advance and as her personal circumstances grew worse and worse she didn't seem to have the strength to tackle much work at all.

I grew accustomed to mucking out and strapping the horses myself, whilst Rita sat on an upturned bucket, sniffing into a cactus cloth, pouring out her latest catastrophes relating to her imprisoned husband, her social security claims, her delinquent son (on probation for emptying the gas meter) and her various creditors. I was saved, though, from having to move house to get rid of her, because she did a moonlight flit herself. With her bills unpaid and the gas meter agape, she vanished and so did her son. I never saw her again.

Years later, when we first saw Beaker, the laboratory assistant on the Muppet Show, we all shrieked, "It's Rita!" It wasn't, of course, but if Rita is still working as a groom, and if anyone recognises her from my description, be sure to give her my love, and tell her she can keep the rubber boots.

Volunteers Are Sought

No regular follower of this column will be unaware of my sterling efforts to discover a mode of hunting which will be acceptable to all. I have tried the fox hunt; the interminable flogging from blank cover to empty thicket with the good steel shoes and the patience wearing thinner by the minute, and the only run of the day foiled by a member of the Hunt Saboteurs Association with a balaclava, a bicycle and a stink bomb. I have tried the harriers; pounding the headlands in ever decreasing circles, praying for the soul of the landowner who, his face devoid of all expression, stands at the gate and watches fifty horses thunder across his one good meadow for the fourth time in the same morning. I have tried and abandoned the drag hunt; the smelly sausage hauled over the pre-determined route, the furious gallop over thirty-nine five-foot fences and home in time for tea. And I have to admit that I have neither the mettle nor the stomach for the chase of the wild red deer.

But it has not been in vain. Because at last, I bring you the solution to the hunting problem: bloxhounds. Bloxhounds, I assure you, are a hunting person's dream.

A bloxhound is a cross between a foxhound and a bloodhound. It is not, one is forced to admit, the most elegant creature in the world. To a bloodhound–sort–of–person it appears rather squat, unusually open-featured and somewhat oddly marked. To a foxhound–sort–of–person it is disconcertingly large and drab and its coat is several sizes too large; it looks as though it would be vastly improved by a visit to a Top Person's Tailor who, with skill and a mouthful of pins, could take in a few discreet tucks here and there. But the value of the bloxhound has nothing at all to do with its looks, because it is entirely redeemed by the excellence of its nose.

The nose of the bloxhound is truly amazing. Students of the chase can replace the Beckfords, the Budgetts and the Pollards upon the library shelves. Their scentometers are redundant: the bloxhound has an olfactory sense second to none. There will be no more hours spent beside the dripping spinney with the hands set fast upon the reins and the water trickling off the horse's chin; the check which halts the proceedings just long enough for you to get out your sandwiches, only to see them trampled underfoot in the rush to be away again, is already a thing of the past. The bloxhound will change your life.

Next to its nose (which, it has to be said, is not greatly impressive to look at, being black and moist with two holes, surrounded by wobbly, pinch–pleated folds of skin), the most celebratory virtue of this truly wonderful canine is that it does not kill its quarry. In fact it had better not, because its quarry is not an animal, not even a vegetable, but a human. And the penalty for tearing a human to shreds being what it is, the huntsman had better not let it do so. There, the secret is out.

Imagine now, the delight of the League Against Cruel Sports, the joy of the Hunt Saboteurs Association, upon receipt of such news. As one man they will clasp every Master of Foxhounds in the land to their bosoms with relief and affection. They will appear at the meets scattering rose petals under the feet of the horses. At the Bloxhound

Ball they will join in the horn blowing competitions and the Post Horn Gallop and their president will be given the seat next to Prince Charles.

There is only one minor difficulty, a trifling matter to be settled before packs of bloxhounds are introduced all over the country. A tiny question mark is hanging over the Revolution of Hunting As We Know It. It is this. To the best of our belief, bloxhounds do not eat people. At least, they have not eaten a single person up until the moment of writing, but then they haven't managed to catch one yet. Our volunteers, being extremely fleet of foot, have not been keen to put it to the test. Nobody can quite understand why.

The temperament of the bloxhound is impeccable. His manners are beyond reproach. In truth, he is a jolly, friendly, companionable chap, helpful, obedient, and eager to please. His intelligence is second to none. But though all hasten to agree that the bloxhound is a happy, laughing, affectionate fellow on his own, it is only fair to state that he may not be quite himself when part of the baying pack. Nobody has let him get close enough to find out.

This, dear readers, is where you come in. Volunteers of the most sporting variety are sought to test the only pack of bloxhounds in the country. Bloxhounds are straining at their couples, the horses are saddled, the flasks are brimming with the finest brandy, the sandwiches are cut. Write and offer yourselves in your legions. I know, I just know, you won't fail me.

To Knowledgeable Home Only . . .

The pony I have just been describing as a paragon of equine virtue, atom-bomb-proof and a suitable mount for a babe-in-arms, suddenly tucks its tail between its legs, puts in an almighty buck and sets off up the field like a jerboa with its child rider only partially adhering to the saddle. I turn to the parents with a tremulous smile and a perplexed shrug of the shoulders, intending to convey that this behaviour is so totally unexpected, so completely out of character, that it renders me speechless, but probably conveying nothing of the sort. One might imagine that, after all these years, selling off one's surplus equines would be as easy as falling off over a log, but it isn't, and cordial relations are somewhat strained as I escort the waxen-faced trio back to their car.

There have been worse experiences than this. Take for instance, the sale of the flying machine. The flying machine was very beautiful in a dashing, romantic sort of way. He was the kind of horse portrayed in old hunting prints as galloping fearlessly across Leicestershire turf, having crashing falls at every fence. His bravery was beyond question, but his jumping ability was appalling, and the speed at which he took his fences had one's heart in one's mouth. Nevertheless, retired from the chase and schooled in basic jumping technique, I advertised him for sale. *Big, bold, chestnut gelding, seven years. Potential eventer or Point-to-Pointer. Hunted to date by a lady.*

The charming family who fell for the flying machine bore him off in glory, bound for the world of the Three-Day Event, at almost twice the price I had paid for him. This might have been the Sale of the Century, but for what happened next.

The very next morning he was led out of his stable and found to have only three legs. The other one just hung there and dangled.

The vet and I arrived at the yard in the same cloud of dust. I jumped out of the Land Rover clutching my unpresented cheque and my cancelled insurance policy, and he jumped out of his shooting brake with his humane killer cocked and loaded. We hit the stable door together. The flying machine stood four-square on the straw with a surprised expression on his face and a wisp of straw sticking out of the side of his mouth. I had to have brandy poured down my throat when I was told he had just temporarily slipped his stifle out of joint.

For some time I conducted my horse-dealing activities from a village pub, where startled diners were in danger of being whisked out to the stables to view my latest wares between courses, and where waitresses would whip off their aprons and hop into the saddle to display their paces round the car park. Sue and I divided our time between the stables, the bars, and the kitchen; so while Elaine, whose horse was at livery in the yard, might be describing a show-jumping course she had negotiated, using grissini to construct replica obstacles on the kitchen table, Sue would be thumping steak or arranging snails in a dish, and I might be consoling a diner who had found an aphid on his lettuce. Sometimes, if our interests overlapped and we didn't have time to change, we rushed around in breeches and boots, juggling soups; and because it was a horsy place, with hunting prints and foxes' masks hanging up, customers assumed it was some kind of weird uniform for staff.

Dealing in horses from a pub though, was not always good for business. One day I was surprised over the duck pâté by the vet, and a customer happened to glance out of the window and saw me running a horse up the road in my striped apron, in order to display a pronounced lameness. "Is that the cook?" he enquired of the barman. The barman agreed that it probably was. "In that case," the customer said hastily, "I'll change my order for a meat pie to a cheese salad!"

Another sale which lingers in my memory is the one which involved the New Forest pony. When we first took delivery of him we didn't have him shod, not through reasons of economy but through reasons of safety; the pony being rather likely to trample us underfoot after he had slung, squashed or scraped us off (and by 'we', you will understand that I mean Sue, because all the time he was in the yard I neatly avoided ever having to place my foot in his stirrup).

Working without shoes had the beneficial effect of rendering his feet like iron, and even when his schooling was complete and he was ready for sale, we saw no reason ever to have him shod. It was actually a pleasure to reduce the price a little, so that he could go to an eager child whose careworn mother had saved the money from her housekeeping. All went well on the day of delivery; the fenced paddock, the field shelter and the water supply were satisfactory; the enthusiasm and the joy of the proud new owner were beyond question. But came the dusk a belligerent male voice on the telephone demanded, " 'Ere, what d'yer mean, sellin' my gal an 'orse wiv no 'oofs on?"

Careful explanations followed, but unplaced, the irate parent faded out on a mutter. "Never 'eard anyfink like it, sellin' an 'orse wiv no 'oofs on . . ." Only a few minutes later the careworn mother rang to inform us in a whisper that her husband thought all ponies were born with shoes attached, adding, "He's a bit fond of the bottle, so he's not quite *himself*, if you see what I mean."

Living and working in a pub, we did!

Too High Off the Ground, Actually

In the publicity handout for *Eventer's Dream*, I found stated, quite clearly and brazenly, for all the world to see, that I was once the proprietor of the Worst Riding School in the World. Since, sometime in the foggy past, I must have provided my publishers with the information for the handout myself, I supposed that this must be almost true, as all publishers' handouts and dustwrapper blurbs written by authors about themselves are invariably nearly the truth.

Nevertheless, it is a shock to the system to see it so uncompromisingly stated.

The whole truth of the matter is that the riding school in question was started by myself as a mere infant of eighteen years, with the support of two friends, on little more than a passion for horses and a steely determination to toil for none but ourselves.

Together we painted miles of post and rail fencing, laid hardcore and filthy, black ash for a manege, renovated and whitewashed dilapidated stabling, then looked in our bank accounts for the wherewithal to buy horses and discovered that there was not.

We took liveries at first and schooled ponies. RIDING LESSONS proclaimed our uneven, hand-lettered sign, and underneath in smaller letters, 'on your own horse'. Not surprisingly, our clients were few and far between to start with, and in our early days we earned more from selling horse manure by the bag than from instructing people in the Art of Horse(wo)manship.

We used to deliver our manure locally, stuffed into the paper sacks that our pony nuts were delivered in. This was all right when it was dry, but more tricky when it was wet because they got jolly heavy.

Sometimes, delivering to the terraced rows in Burton-on-Trent where there was only one narrow tunnel of an entry leading to the back gardens of about twelve houses, the occupants would take pity on us and let us heave our bags in through the front door, over the carpets, and out through the back. We lost our nerve though, when the bottom fell out of a bag in somebody's sitting room right in front of the television set.

By degrees the riding school established itself. We were the last resort of the part-livery brigade, the people who schooled and broke the equine characters the other establishments wouldn't touch with a barge pole (we knew all about barge poles because we were on the canal in Burton-on-Trent), and by degrees we achieved a basic equine stock, sub-standard and imperfect, but purchased for peanuts, because peanuts were all there was.

"Good Heavens," the Inspector from the Association of British Riding Schools exclaimed when she was summoned to inspect our premises for approval. "Don't you have any sound animals on the place at *all*?"

"Certainly," we replied, producing a fine chestnut and positioning it with care so that the good eye was on her side. For the rest, ringbone, roarers, arthritics, crib-biters, double heartbeats, sweet-itch, we had them all. The only thing to impress the lady from the ABRS was our medicine chest, which excelled in size and content anything she had ever experienced before. After some heart-searching she put us on the list of probationary members, but not before one of us had looked over her shoulder and read what she had written about our establishment in her notebook. *Stock suspect, if not actually unsound. Stable management generally good. Instruction ineffective but probably harmless.*

Of all these things it was the *Instruction ineffective but probably harmless* which touched a raw nerve, because as instructors in the Art of Horse(wo)manship, we had considered ourselves pretty hot stuff. Much agonising followed, after which it was decided that one of us would have to go to a Top Class Establishment, to find out how it should be done, and then come back and teach the other two; and as I was supposed to be the proprietor it had better be me.

I was quite pleased about this, but when I saw the prospectus sent by the Top Class Establishment I immediately got cold feet. It was full of immaculate, determined-looking females riding big, fit thoroughbred horses. I was neither immaculate nor determined, and I had always disliked riding anything over fourteen hands high because of feeling Too High Off the Ground. My fears were well founded.

. . . immaculate, determined-looking females riding big fit horses

From the very first day I loathed the big, fit thoroughbred horses, who sniffed out my anxiety in the first five minutes and rarely missed an opportunity to show who really had the upper hand. Worse, not only did I find myself Too High Off the Ground, but also Completely Off the Ground; they were very into jumping at the Top Class Establishment.

The whole class of students would stand in a line facing a row of jumps in various combinations, and the instructor would yap us over them one by one. Since I had never been able to approach a jump save in a suicidal dive with my eyes tightly shut and knuckles showing white on the reins, I got very good at slipping to the end of the queue when it was almost my turn.

My jumping improved hardly at all, but I learned something of equal value; I learned how to say *Actually*. The students at the Top Class Establishment were very posh. They had the sort of parents who were perfectly happy to let their daughters fiddle about with horses as a kind of further education, using the Top Class Establishment as a kind of finishing school where they could mix with the 'right sort' of people.

The posh students were simply amazed that I was learning for three and they couldn't believe I had never heard of smoked salmon, Sammy Davis Junior and Hermes headscarves. I was equally amazed to discover that they didn't envisage ever having to use the knowledge they were acquiring to support themselves; that earning a living wage was something Other People (meaning the working classes) worried about. In fact, they were the vanguard of that dying breed, the 'Show Jumpers Salvation' – the "pound a week and see the world" brigade.

Actually was a great social asset when I got home. Nobody ever said *actually* in Burton–on–Trent. When I started to teach the other two, I taught them that as well. Our powers of Instructing in the Art of Horse(wo)manship may not have improved very much, but we got marvellously good at saying *actually*.

We're still saying it, actually.

Point-to-Point

In my riding school days someone conceived the idea of taking a coach load of the younger element to the local Point-to-Point. I was in charge of the outing and all was going well. The pupils, having commandeered a hay cart near the finishing post, were doing their level best to make sure no horses finished the course.

At the appointed hour I waited by the coach with the driver, ready for the return journey. Not a soul arrived. Eventually it was revealed that in the last race of the day, two fences from home, a horse had come down awkwardly and broken a leg. Like angels of mercy the pupils had flown to the scene of the accident and stayed, despite much official shooing, until the decidedly bitter end. All the way home they wept and cried and wailed. Nobody drank the crates of lemonade and the working pupils lived on potato crisps for weeks afterwards.

Naturally, the parents of the pupils blamed me for the repercussions; the lost appetites and the screams in the night; and two children gave up riding altogether, marked for life.

This traumatic experience may have coloured my own feelings towards the Point-to-Point which, one has to admit, are less than enthusiastic. The weather is another stumbling block. It's all very well for the owners and riders, they have their nerves to keep them warm, but I never am; even all the dashing backwards and forwards from the Tote to the course does nothing to thaw my frozen extremities.

Seasoned Point-to-Pointers are a hardy lot, all that standing about waiting for hounds to break cover hardens them off; but I can't think of anything more uncomfortable than standing on some exposed piece of ground in a freezing gale, encased in a sheepskin jacket (the next best thing I know to a straitjacket – although the comparison, I would like you to know, does not emanate from personal experience), sipping the thin miscellaneous soup served up on these occasions whilst the hunting fraternity mill about, clapping each other jovially on the back, exchanging hot tips, hip flasks and the odd wife, whilst the hunt supporters' club rattle tins under one's leaking nose for the Poultry Fund or the British Field Sports Society.

On one memorable occasion I was actually offered a ride in a Point-to-Point by someone who, having only slight knowledge himself, was not really in a position to know better.

By this time I was past my prime, having given up riding schools and even the Art of Horse(wo)manship, in order to produce small ponies for the show ring. My friends, when I told them about the Point-to-Point offer, were felled as one man by the jest. "What," they cried, "doesn't he know you never ride anything over twelve hands high? Doesn't he know you lead your ponies from a bicycle because you've lost your nerve? Didn't he see you fall off the child's first pony in the collecting ring at Derby County?"

Huffily, I replied that they may yet be forced to eat their words and I arranged to go and inspect the Point-to-Pointer. The sight of it brought me out in a cold sweat. It was almost seventeen hands and coal black in every part. It had small white-rimmed eyes and a piece out of one ear reminiscent of a tom cat who had been in a fight. When it saw me coming across the yard it began to snake its head up and down, rattling its teeth and flattening its ears on its neck. Obviously it would have weaved a greeting had it been possible, because on each side of its head hung a device consisting of two house bricks with holes bored in them, suspended in the air by means of baler twine. As I approached, it let fly with a succession of rapid kicks at the back of the stable which sounded like gunfire. It was not exactly a promising start.

"He'll be a bit of a handful in the hunting field, I don't doubt," the owner said modestly, as he fenced the coal black horse with a headcollar. "But if you qualify him, I'll pay your expenses." He managed to attach the headcollar to the horse's head and, clinging to the headcollar rope, was carried out of the stable and round the yard, helpless as a leaf on the wind.

It hadn't dawned on me that I would be expected to qualify the horse. I had enjoyed vague visions of being legged up in the paddock in the silks with the hoops and the stripe, being led sedately down to the start, loosed as the starter dropped the white flag, and being neatly caught at the other end as I arrived past the finishing post (first, naturally), in order to receive a gold-plated cup whilst the man from *Horse & Hound* took my photograph. Surveying the coal black horse plunging round the yard before me, I could foresee a stickier, decidedly nastier, end.

I declined the Point-to-Point ride, pointing out that my recent experiences centred around the show pony world which, for all its charm, was not exactly the Sporting Life. The next time I saw the coal black horse it was out with the Meynell and its rider, a casually dressed youth flourishing a mighty ash plant, was being rated by the huntsman for allowing the brute to tread on a hound.

I was mightily glad it wasn't me.

Ride or Drive

The Art of Driving has many disciples. Given half a chance they will break their shaft stops to impress upon you how stylish and mettlesome is the horse in harness, how skilled and artistic is the whip, and how generally great are the advantages, both visual and practical, of driving, over the mere bestriding, of horses.

It is both difficult and foolish to argue, because, of course, there are advantages. The first is that you can wear a feather in your hat without looking a fool and the second is that, as when reading the News at Ten, you can wear the most shocking things below the belt as long as your top half remains true to conventional good taste.

From the above it will be deduced that I am not a driving enthusiast. The truth of the matter is that I am more the mistress on top of a horse than attached to its behind and, after a lifetime of aspiring to the Art of Horse(wo)manship, it is unnerving to have nothing between your knees when things threaten to get out of control.

I have had more than a nodding acquaintance with the Art of Driving. In my youth I spent many Sundays collecting pig-swill with a pony and cart and my best friend, Christine. The pig-swill bins gave forth a powerful smell and on warm days we were obliged to walk in front or behind the cart to escape the sickening pong. The pony didn't mind as he was ex-Ivanhoe Dairies and much preferred being left to his own devices; in fact once we started to interfere with the reins we seemed to hit the kerb rather a lot.

Then there was Thunder. Thunder was a piebald cob, sold to me in my riding school days as a ride and drive. It didn't take long to get tired of the ride, because the horse was a sluggard at the walk, unstoppable at the trot, and permanently disunited at the canter (he refused to gallop altogether). There seemed little else for it but to test the drive. As we had no equipage of our own, we took him to a local driving expert called Jack Sheppard. Jack Sheppard harnessed the horse and put him to a cart. The piebald cob stood like a rock throughout, inspiring Jack Sheppard with such confidence that he saw us all aboard the vehicle as the horse shouldered the collar and pulled us out of the yard as sweetly as a lamb. It was only when he reached the meadow and perceived that there was something following inexorably behind him that he took offence. Up went the cob's hogged neck, back went his ears and off he set across the grass at a scorching trot with his passengers clinging to the sides of the swaying, bouncing cart like survivors to a raft. When this activity failed to disencumber him, he dropped anchor in a mightily abrupt manner and proceeded to kick the cart to pieces. With the sound of splintering wood and Jack Sheppard's curses ringing in our ears we made our retreat, painfully aware that we had yet another totally useless animal on our hands.

If one horse attached to a vehicle can wreak such havoc, consider four. My mistake, before clambering onto the Norwich Union Mercury Mail Coach on an assignment for *Light Horse*, lay in considering overmuch. I was armed to the teeth with historic information; none of it reassuring. I knew, for instance, that in 1836 the presence of a stone in the road had so jolted the Dartmoor Mail that the coachman and the guard had toppled from their seats, leaving a solitary innocent passenger alone with the galloping horses. I also remembered, as a numbing chill crept up my sleeves and my cheeks stiffened in the freezing wind, that on such a journey two out of three outside passengers on the Bath coach were found to be frozen to death on arrival at their destination . . .

Four In Hand

He promised me snow, instead I get ice. I appreciate it is the best he can do at short notice, but it makes me nervous about the horses. The Norfolk lanes are narrow and hilly in parts; there are high hedges guarding patches of frozen water, where the sun can never reach. For reassurance, I am shown the single, mordax stud screwed into the outside heel of each of the four, grey, Hungarian horses, but still I clamber to the top of the two-ton coach feeling that never has so much depended on so little.

This coach, as well as being potentially hazardous, is historic. It was known to be carrying mail until it was auctioned in 1886 and one of its previous owners went down with the *Lusitania*. James Selby, the celebrated coachman, is thought to have driven it in his heyday when, after he had driven 108 miles in seven and a half hours for a wager of a thousand pounds (although rumour has it that he never saw the money), people paid double fares for the privilege of riding with him. Selby died as a result of exposure on top of a coach and in 1881, driving from Windsor to London, his hat froze to his head and had to be thawed off by pouring hot water round the brim.

John Parker, former coachman to the Royal Army Service Corps and more recently, to the Norwich Union Insurance Company, is full of jolly little stories like this; lantern-jawed and lugubrious, in his camel top coat and hat with chocolate trimmings, he is definitely a period piece; and he can see that I have forgotten my gloves.

In order not to spoil the photographs, I have been obliged to strip off my Husky waistcoat and jacket and put on a velvet coat. The coat is two sizes smaller than me and the straw hat with the flowers and the dangling ribbons seems unseasonable wear for November. I envy Colin Page, the Norwich Union Publicity Manager, his fur-lined coat, but not his dented top hat; and at least, sitting in front of the box seat, he keeps the worst of the wind off me.

The mail coach, blessed, restored and sponsored by the Norwich Union, gleams in the winter sunshine as the rugs are taken off the horses and the chocks are pulled away from the wheels. You can see your face in the paint, and the brass fittings knock your eye out – all this after 3,000 miles with the horses and 20,000 in motor transit. The horses, shaking their heads and stamping their feet, anxious to be away, are magnificent beasts of sixteen hands, branded on the neck with the initials of their stud; their coats are laundry-bright, their hooves are oiled; their black patent harness is made-to-measure by Susan Townshend.

Susan, accomplished saddler, whip and riding instructress, takes up her position behind on the extra seats added by the Post Office to help combat inflation in the Golden Age; with her are Carole and Isobel, and Fudge, the one-eyed spaniel. The girls are resplendent in spanking white breeches and cravats, top hats and frock coats. They are ever ready to leap off and pound to the front of the horses in the event of a disaster or diversion. The thought, to a person of small courage, is almost a comfort.

Sitting next to me on the cushioned bench seat with the rail behind to prevent passengers from falling off backwards when the horses set off unexpectedly (which they do now with a frightening lurch accompanied by a hideous cacophony of hooves and wheels), is a nice-looking young man with an even more dented top hat and a comforting manner. His name is Malcolm and after I have recovered from the shock of moving off, and been advised to cram the straw hat down to my ears to prevent it being swept away by the over-hanging branches, Malcolm tells me about the Great Mail Coach Run from

. . . a little, black-lined box

Norwich to Antwerp; how they had special permission to drive straight through the Customs' Hall and onto the docks at Felixstowe; how the trams in Brussels whipped past at thirty miles an hour, twelve inches from the wheels; how the wheels got stuck in the tram lines; how the police stopped all the traffic to allow them safe passage, and the Burgomaster received them at the Hotel de Ville after the Hungarians had risked life and limb to skate across the giant cobbles to the Grande Place. It is a relief to know that the man on the box seat has endured all this without mishap.

Inside the coach it is like riding in a little, black-lined box. The seats are narrow and it seems impossible that four people ever travelled long distances cooped up like this. On the bonus side, it is possible to pull up the little windows and shut out the weather, the noise and the world; then you can generate a good, unhealthy fug. Intimate is the only word for it.

But it is best on top, even at the risk of freezing to death. The coachman's layered coat, his steady voice encouraging the horses, the rhythmic swinging of four dappled rumps, the sun catching at the brass, the steady lap-lap of white manes, the pricked ears of the leaders and the wide road opening out ahead, are pure intoxication.

Travel by coach is perhaps more comfortable than one might expect; coaches were, after all, built for rougher roads than these. Progress though, since the days of tarmacadam, is accompanied by a great deal of noise – the rumbling of metal-hooped wheels, the grating of the brakes applied when going downhill, the crashing of sixteen trotting hooves shod with mild steel. This coach is accorded much the same reception as in days gone by; heads poke out of cottage windows; villagers wave from their garden gates. Motorists on the wide road slow down to a crawl, pink-faced with excitement. Encountered in a narrow lane, they grow pale and, crashing their gears, reverse away at top speed, wild-eyed.

As we turn off the road into Wingfield Common, the clatter of our progress stops abruptly to be replaced by other, gentler noises – the familiar soft thud of hooves on grass, the jingle of harness, the creak of woodwork; the sight of us sends the ponies spinning round their tethers like tops.

We trot round and past the castle so that there can be photographs; the photographer runs about, popping up in unexpected places and making the leaders shy. Overcome by the excitement of it all, I ask if there is a post horn. John Parker says there isn't, not today. His expression enquires what more am I likely to ask for.

Back at Swingletree Stables, John Parker pulls off his glove and shows me his hand where he has been holding the reins. From the first knuckle upwards it is completely bloodless and set fast. He can't move his fingers; he has iced up. "And that's only the start of it. After a bit it starts to creep up your arm and into your shoulders; people were killed when it happened in the old days, the coach ran over or into anything that happened to be in its path, pedestrians, animals, other vehicles. The coachman couldn't do a thing about it; he was paralysed." He rubs his frozen hands and looks dismal. Standing by his horses in his deep layered top coat he could have stepped out of a Christmas card by Cecil Aldin. "Roll on Olympia," he says. "I shall be warm for a week."

The Donkeys' Day

Dispatched to cover the Donkey Breed Society's Annual Show at Malvern by *Riding* (a gesture of confidence they later had cause to regret), and accustomed as I was to reporting on horse shows, I made a fatal mistake. I failed to take it seriously.

I thought I knew about donkeys. In my youth I had been acquainted with many of the beach variety. In Skegness where, as I remember it, the sun always shone down from a cloudless blue sky and the sand was hot under one's feet, they stood about in little groups amongst the deck chairs and drooped their heads; or they ran along the tideline, just out of range of the inevitable boy and his stick, whilst shrieking bathers clung to the leaping heads of their redundant side-saddles.

Since then, as I was to discover, there had been a major change in the donkey's status; he had been adopted by the Best People. He had been schooled and groomed for stardom.

At the donkey show, catalogued exhibits with names like Kittoch-hill Wester of Glan Aber, stood two to a stable, demure and solemn in initialled rugs and tail bandages, or stood singly between camp beds and groceries, wheezing a domestic greeting as one peered over the door.

In the grand arena, donkey colts reinforced their dislike of the weather (notably a force ten gale) and their reluctance to show their paces with tortured braying, reducing nattily-dressed judges and bowler-hatted attendants to whimsy. In the jumping ring, donkey show-jumpers ran round or through six-inch obstacles (a painted cloth wall, a brush stuffed with flowering heather), thus proving you don't actually realise what a donkey can't do until you see it trying. One anguished competitor fled the ring and dived unbid into the members' tent; and in the handy donkey competition another made his feelings known by uttering an indignant rasp and lying down.

All of this I regarded with genuine wonder as I struggled to walk against the wind and hold onto my notes; as bowler hats, catalogues and rosettes hurtled across the ground at alarming speeds with their owners in determined pursuit. I couldn't help feeling that it was perhaps all a bit much to endure for one so recently dragged in from the orchard; promoted from docile companion and beach buggy to Top Person's status symbol with a healthy service industry mush-rooming around him since he must now be registered, rugged, harnessed, attached to a cart, groomed and clipped like a hunter, fed special donkey foods and vitamin supplements, whilst his owners must be furnished with donkey ties, donkey pictures, donkey ornaments, donkey jewellery, must subscribe to donkey charities and dry their dishes on donkey printed glass cloths. It was all a far, far cry from Queenie in Skegness whose only claim to fame was that she could traverse her sixpenny route even when her outsize browband (painted in red gloss with her name picked out in white) dropped down over her eyes.

The weather which, as one of the irate correspondents to the editor after the report appeared was to point out, might have defeated a less stout-hearted gathering, has yet to be matched in my experience, and just as I was about to begin my lunch there was an ominous crack and part of the marquee took off.

To urgent cries of, "Everybody OUT!" we fled. Most had the presence of mind to gather up their food but when I got outside all I had was my knife and fork gripped firmly in either hand. This necessitated a foray into the flapping, fluttering remains to rescue my lunch, which seemed preferable to going without it. En route to my car which seemed the safest retreat, my glass of wine blew away and so did my bread roll. Tablecloths flew away and draped themselves over trees and hedges, and Photonews were stunned by the collapse of their own banner. The marquee was poised for flight like a gigantic kite but the Donkey Breed Society were made of strong stuff. In a trice they had organised a chain of human volunteers to rescue the alcoholic beverages and not long afterwards they had collapsed the ballooning mass of canvas below what looked like the drunken masts and rigging of a shipwreck. One of the press reporters regarded the evacuated beer crates with satisfaction. "That's what I like to see," he said. "Somebody with their priorities right."

When the show report finally appeared, the editor's mail suddenly increased twofold and my name was, once again, mud. Amongst others, Major Chetwynd Talbot accused me of sneering at the "peak condition and turnout" of donkeys on their day, and Lady Monica Sternberg told me off roundly for my "snide remarks", insisting that donkeys would remain family pets not "poor man's ponies", and that their owners have a sense of humour not usually associated with the show pony world.

Reeling from the onslaught of the furious letters, I was not inclined to agree.

A Donkey's Downfall

When my husband bought him, I could think of a lot of reasons why, just at that particular moment, we didn't need a donkey.

Lack of grazing was one.

"They live on nettles," he said.

Lung worm was another.

"Panic writing," he said, dismissively.

"How old is it?" I asked.

"Quite a little one really," he said, evasively.

"What sex is it?" I asked.

"I didn't think to ask," he admitted.

"If it's a jack," I said. "It will have to be gelded."

My donkey-loving husband grew pale and looked as though he might faint. "It'll be a girl," he said. It wasn't.

Our donkey arrived and the breeder of the donkey delivered it; she was slim and attractive and had long dark hair. The ponies glared at the donkey. I glared at my husband. The breeder smiled and pocketed the money. My husband went to the library and borrowed a book on

. . . donkeys are friendly, sociable animals

donkey-keeping; the first thing he learned was that they didn't live on nettles.

"Donkeys," said the book, "are friendly, sociable animals."

We couldn't get near ours. He watched our approach warily, flipped his enormous ears backwards and forwards a few times, then cantered off. He took an instant dislike to our dogs, chasing them furiously out of the paddock if they dared to enter, and if they chanced to be near enough, he tried to stamp on them. He commandeered the field shelter and refused to let the ponies enter it; when it rained they stood outside and looked mournful.

"Donkeys are lovable pets and are wonderful with children," said the book. To be truthful, our donkey never damaged a child although in his time he took a piece out of my thigh, knocked my husband into the hedge (serve him right), and kicked the dogs, the ponies and the blacksmith.

"Donkeys do not need breaking-in," the book informed us. A friend of ours disproved this theory by jumping on, admittedly unexpectedly and from behind. Our donkey fled bucking up the field, depositing him in no uncertain manner. Nobody can catch our donkey. It is lured into the stables with a bowl of pony nuts ("Not suitable for donkeys," the book said). Luring into the stables is effected most weekends and whenever else there is an interment in the churchyard with which we share a common fence. Our donkey is fascinated by burials, whether drawn by the floral tributes or the sombre mourners it is hard to tell, but his vocal encouragement occasioned an indignant visit from the rector.

When the flies were gone and the autumn arrived, so did the veterinary surgeon. He stepped from his car and donned a vast rubber apron and thigh boots. I had lured our donkey into the stable the previous evening and starved him as instructed; this morning I had been unable to meet his eyes and I now hoped that my part in the proceedings was over. "Can I go now?" I said nervously as, neatly tied up in his rubber suit, the vet took some fearful looking implements from the back of his car.

"Go?" he said, looking astonished. "Didn't they tell you I should want you to assist?"

I said *they* hadn't; that I couldn't; that I should be sick or faint. Already I could feel my legs begin to weaken.

"You better not," he said unfeelingly. "I've only come prepared to treat the donkey; I've nothing for fainting females."

We cornered the donkey and managed to get a headcollar on and an injection in. When we let him go he stared at us accusingly for a few seconds then he swayed, staggered, and fell onto a pile of straw neatly pushed under him by the vet.

Our donkey looked very sweet lying there on the floor. "He isn't dead is he?" I asked. "We wouldn't like anything to happen to him."

"If he's still breathing, he's alive," the vet said. "Just sit on his head and hold the end of this rope nice and steady."

"I've changed my mind," I said. "I don't want it done." I sat on our donkey's neck with my eyelids pressed tightly shut.

"Don't do it," I said.

"Too late," he said. "It's done."

"It can't be!" I said, opening my eyes in disbelief and seeing that it was.

Two injections and as many minutes later, our donkey was standing up. Within an hour he had emptied his hay net and two days later he was back in the paddock terrorising the ponies. After a week the slight stiffness had vanished and he was kicking out at the dogs as energetically as usual.

My husband, who had expected a miraculous and beneficial change of personality in our donkey after the operation, was mystified to find that he was still the same as before. He was disappointed and rather disillusioned; he suggested that we might sell him.

In the end it was me who refused to part with him; after all he was a very difficult donkey, not at all typical of the species; how could one possibly word a truthful advertisement, and even if one managed it, who would buy him? What kind of a fool would ever allow himself to be persuaded to part with hard-earned cash in return for such a creature?

"Who indeed?" my husband agreed as, avoiding my steely gaze, he busied himself with his newspaper.

A Sideways Look . . .

I first became interested in riding side-saddle when somebody casually mentioned that it was supposed to be practically impossible to fall off. I had been waiting all my life for a saddle it was not possible to fall out of and my imagination immediately took flight. I saw the side-saddle as the magic answer to all my problems in my struggle to master the Art of Horse(wo)manship as, filled with a new and wonderful courage and firmly attached to the saddle of my dreams, I galloped elegantly towards new horizons.

A delightful lady in the Meynell country, who had shown hunters in her youth with unequalled success, thought she had a good habit left which might fit me. The habit was still in its Roberts & Carroll box, swathed in tissue paper. The jacket was black and heavy with a stunningly cut-away front and Meynell Hunt buttons. I struggled into it. The sleeves were so tapered that I couldn't bend my arms and when I fastened the single button I couldn't breathe. What a pity, my adviser sighed, that it was too small. I denied it. I said that when I had taken off my cardigan, my blouse and my vest, it would be perfect. My adviser looked at me doubtfully; she thought it was a tiny bit short. I took off my shoes and stooped. I felt that it had to fit, I simply couldn't bear to leave without it. Eventually, to placate me, she was forced to agree that perhaps it did fit; well, almost, and having agreed on the jacket, she produced the apron.

The side-saddle apron is a frightening garment. I put it on and discovered that there was no back in it. I stared at my exposed anatomy in the greatest alarm. I enquired if the large hump sticking out in front was normal. My adviser said it was; my knee and the pommel would fit neatly into it, and there was also room for the leaping head. I didn't like the sound of the leaping head; I didn't like the black breeches either, people would think I belonged to the Mounted Police, but I cheered up when I saw the waistcoat, the hat and the veil. Driving home with the box containing the side-saddle habit on the back seat I felt that femininity and romanticism were about to make a welcome return to my life.

All this happened before the great side-saddle revival, and my advertisements for a saddle brought no response. Eventually it was Christine who found one – in an antique shop. It was a monster of a saddle and fearfully heavy, but it had a comfortable-looking dip in the middle of the seat. The antique dealer parted with it reluctantly, he said he had been intending to make it into a stool for the Empress of Austria. (Later it transpired that the Empress of Austria was a pub down the road, but we were much impressed at the 'time.)

Having at length procured a saddle and an aged and partially incomplete book on the Art of the Side-Saddle, I was ready to begin – almost. None of the horses in the yard appeared to fit under the saddle at all; it seemed to have been made for an elephant and it covered everything we put it on from withers to rump. As it happened the mare with the longest back belonged to Christine. She was an old thoroughbred of about fifteen hands with a placid and melancholy disposition and with some reluctance Christine agreed to allow me to try the saddle out on her, on condition that if I damaged the horse, I should have to buy her another. I agreed readily.

The mare backed away and flattened her ears as we trundled the side-saddle into the stable, and when we led her outside, she looked very odd indeed. The saddle sat up at an astonishing height and it didn't seem to clasp her sides at all, despite a frightening array of girths and a balance strap. However, we peered through the front arch, and through a tunnel of Dartford dimensions, we saw daylight; we felt confident that as long as the saddle cleared her spine, all would be well.

The first and only lesson at home was a disaster. Christine, positioned in the middle of the paddock, shouted out instructions in quaint, antiquated language from the book, whose incomplete and browned pages fluttered intermittently to the ground like falling leaves. This made the Art of the Side-Saddle very difficult to grasp indeed, coupled with the antics of the old thoroughbred mare, who when she wasn't walking crab-wise away from my one leg, humped her back and walked on tiptoe like a dromedary. Finally, she became rather bored and relaxed sufficiently to loosen the array of girths, whereupon, under Christine's disbelieving gaze, I slowly and inevitably disappeared down the side of the horse like the setting sun.

The only possible course of action left to me was to enrol for a course of lessons with an expert. Nowadays this would pose no problem as a whispered enquiry would bring the Side-Saddle Association galloping serenely to one's aid, but no such help was forthcoming to me. It was only with the greatest difficulty that I managed to locate someone capable of instruction in the Art of the Side-Saddle, and when I arrived at the establishment I found myself an object of wonder and curiosity amongst the trainee students who hid themselves behind bushes and show-jumps in order to follow my progress without the knowledge of the proprietor; all of which impaired my concentration and made the horse extremely nervous.

I found the prancing, bay arab and the small, straight-seated saddle alarming and precarious; far from being impossible to fall out of, I felt that anything and everything threatened my security. My instructress, white-haired and softly spoken, endured my nervous protests with a gentle smile which cloaked an iron determination to lick me into shape. After the first half hour, she left me alone on the prancing arab and re-appeared with what, in my over-wrought state, I imagined was the head of a slaughtered beast. It turned out to be a small but exceedingly heavy sandbag with the ends tied like lop ears. With this appendage dangling from my right arm, I was drilled unmercifully for three days.

I never did completely master the Art of the Side-Saddle and the romance and femininity which it was to have brought into my life failed to appear. Several years later though, when I was being measured for a riding jacket at Moss Bros., the fitter remarked that one of my arms was quite one inch longer than the other.

A Matching Pair

One day I decided to get myself a show hack. My family were doubtful: "It will cost too much money," they said. My friends were sceptical: "You will never be able to ride it," they said. Unable to ignore the truth inherent in both statements, I decided to compromise. I would start out with an old, experienced horse, a schoolmaster well versed in the craft of the show ring. Later on I would progress to a younger, more beautiful animal which, naturally, would take the showing world by storm.

I advertised for a suitable schoolmaster hack and, since I had only one reply, selection was a simple matter. I didn't even feel it necessary to travel half way across the country to view the horse; I had him sent. He was a fourteen-year old gelding with a vast record of successes behind him.

Standing in my stable he looked a rather ordinary, dark bay horse with a star and one white sock. People came and looked at him; they had all heard of him and had seen his name in lights, but they were visibly disappointed with what they saw. They looked at him doubtfully. "Are you sure it is the same horse?" they said.

Up in the attic I hunted through ancient copies of *Horse & Hound*. There he stood, picked out in the spotlight, the dark bay horse with the star and the one white sock, his bridle hung with rosettes. "Ten years ago is a long time," everyone said gloomily.

I took my hack out to shows. He behaved impeccably, exactly as a schoolmaster should. People stabbed wildly at their catalogues as we trotted by on the inside of the rails. "My word," they cried in tones of astonishment. "It's old so and so! He must be *ancient*!"

Judges became misty-eyed and sentimental. They patted his neck and told him what a grand old stager he was. "Now, he was what you could *call* a hack," they said. But they never gave him a rosette, not ever.

"Let's face it," my friends said, "he has had his day and you are no rider." There was truth in what they said.

One day I was out exercising when I happened to meet a professional showman whose stables were nearby. His name is well known to all so I shall just call him the professional. We exchanged greetings, after he had looked hard to ascertain that it was really me, having never before seen me mounted on anything over thirteen hands high. After which he looked at my hack. He stared for a long time at the dark bay horse with the star and the one white sock. I stared at his hack, and realised at once that his was a better one than mine; she was younger, of course, but amazingly, she was dark bay with a star and one white sock. "They are a pair!" we exclaimed together.

The professional decided that we should enter the pair class at Windsor. "But you will have to ride side-saddle," he said, "it will enhance the impression of elegance." In his immaculate tack room he showed me a side-saddle by Sowter with a suede seat and a navy canvas cover piped in red.

In his indoor school we put the side-saddle onto my hack. My aged schoolmaster hack, beautifully mannered and suitable for a novice, took a violent dislike to it; he simply couldn't bear it. He was lunged in it, stabled in it, he practically lived with it on his back, but he immediately tried to deposit anyone who dared to sit upon it. Finally, the professional said, "You will have to ride my horse instead." His hack didn't mind the side-saddle a bit, but being younger she was apt to be flighty. The first time I attempted a canter we flew round the indoor school with our speed increasing at every lap, taking the corners like a motor-cycle on a circuit. "You do realise," the professional said wryly when I eventually managed to stop, "that hacks are not supposed to know how to gallop?"

With my old hack beside her and the professional talking me along, the young hack became steady, I remembered how to ride side-saddle, and our performances improved every day. Our figure of eight with a simple change became a masterpiece of stride and timing, our rein-back was smooth and fluent; everyone agreed that there had never been a better pair.

My old hack changed beyond recognition with another horse by his side; his neck arched, his ears went forward, his stride lengthened and he was a star again. Of course, the professional's riding *could* have had something to do with it.

Anxious to look our very best I strapped and polished my hack, I burnished the bridle and the professional's beautiful Sowter saddle to a high gloss, and I took my side-saddle habit to the dry-cleaners.

From where I lived Windsor was a long, long drive. The

professional, having hunters and youngstock to show as well as hacks, was there for the week. I drove down on the morning of our class with the Land Rover and trailer.

The exhibitors' stabling is about a mile away from the show ground at Windsor, so I had been in Home Park fussing over my old hack for quite a while before the professional appeared, immaculate and elegant in his black trousers with a braided stripe, his tail coat and his silk hat; with a red carnation in his buttonhole and another in his leather-gloved hand for me.

I left him with the horses whilst I fled to coil up my hair. I fixed it with pins and a hair net and pulled on my breeches and boots. I put on my shirt and tied my stock, and whilst I fastened the pin with my trembling fingers, I looked round for my habit. I couldn't see it. This was hardly surprising because it was still hanging up at the dry cleaners, swathed in polythene, awaiting my collection.

A great and immediate panic began. Nobody who had ridden in the ladies' hack or hunter classes appeared to be anything like my size. There was not a borrowed habit to be had that didn't drag on the floor, balloon round my waist, or hang six inches beyond my fingertips.

There was a pretty, blonde girl whose habit I tried, but it was far too small. The apron showed six inches of inelegant boot and the jacket strained and gaped across my chest. The professional, not unreasonably, lost his temper. He said it was a ridiculous situation, that I was hopelessly incapable and inefficient, forgetful, stupid and disorganised; and that the pretty, blonde girl would have to ride his horse.

The pretty, blonde girl said she would be delighted. I got out my hack, with his round hard plaits and his coat like satin, and I held him whilst the professional mounted. His mouth was set in a grim line and he didn't look at me. The pretty, blonde girl was put up onto the young hack. I saw that she was a better rider than me, and I watched them ride away down the little avenue of trees towards the collecting ring; towards the band and the flowers and the grandstand. The two dark bay horses, each with a star and one white sock.

I sat in the front of the Land Rover. I couldn't bear to watch the class. I pulled all the pins out of my hair and let them drop to the floor. I put on the radio and I tried not to think of my old horse cantering round the ring on the one last day in his life he was going to be a star.

It seemed a long time before I saw the hacks coming back. The first pair to come trotting along the avenue were dark bays each with a star and a white sock. Red satin rosettes with glittering golden centres fluttered from their bridles.

I should have been pleased perhaps, but I wasn't. I jumped out of the Land Rover, ran across the preliminary judging ring whilst a class was in progress, leaned on the back of the public bar and cried my eyes out.

When I had recovered, I wandered back past the press tent. One of my editors spotted me. "Your horse won the pairs," he said. "We thought you would be riding it." After which he looked at my blotchy face and my puffy eyes and, because editors can read between the lines even when there aren't any lines, he slipped an arm around my shoulders and bought me a very large, very strong drink.

Portrait of a Lady

I've always wanted to be done in oils, and when I saw the advertisement, *Equestrian Portraits – Reasonable terms. Distance no object*, I saw my chance. I rang the artist. I wanted, I said rather grandly, a portrait painted.

"Certainly," he said. "In the academic style perhaps, pensive at the desk with quill in hand and drapes to the rear? Or a domestic setting with child on the knee and dogs gambolling at the feet? Or a head and shoulders in the romantic manner, pink chiffon and pearls?"

"I would like an equestrian portrait," I said firmly; and to minimise further misunderstanding, added, "on a horse."

"Well, naturally," he said.

Disconcerted by the wide range of portrait styles he had to offer, I enquired if he did many equestrian portraits, for, as I was sure he realised, horses were an extremely specialised subject.

"Madam," he replied in a wounded voice, clearly cut to the quick, "no one, but no one, has ever voiced a complaint about the quality of my work, be the subject a person, a poodle or a peony."

I booked him for the following Friday at three o'clock.

I was at this time the possessor of an aged show hack whose fading beauty had once (ridden by a more skilled horsewoman than I, it is true) won him the title of Show Hack of the Year. Of course, he was old by this time; his day of glory had passed, and mine was destined never to arrive. Still, in my optimism, I looked upon him as a springboard, a schoolmaster, from whose clockwork paces, polished and ring-crafty, I would progress to younger, show-stopping horses. On the Friday morning I got my old horse ready.

He regarded his preparation, the tennis-ball plaits, the whiskers trimmed with the bacon scissors, the winter coat laid with spray-on furniture polish, with growing dismay. In his prime he had been to Wembley eight years in succession and his wise old vaselined eyes said, "Oh God, not again!"

I left him in the stable, arching his neck in a very peculiar way, rolling his eyes and opening and shutting his mouth in what appeared to be a mild fit.

I burnished his side-saddle, soaped his bridle, and went to get myself ready. By the time the artist arrived I was resplendent in a well-cut habit of the very best material, my good linen stock, a curly-brimmed bowler hat with a fetchingly patterned veil and, to complete the outfit, a mahogany stick with a silver knob at the end. No one, but no one, was more prepared for posterity than I.

The first thing I noticed about the artist was that he was waving a camera instead of a sketching block. Observing my expression of dismay, he smiled winningly. Everyone, but everyone, worked from photographs these days. No one, but no one, could afford to stand about for hours with a sketch pad. It was the time involved, didn't I understand? Time, he said, holding a little black table-tennis bat up to the sky and squinting into the camera, was of the essence.

I brought out the hack, who stared suspiciously at the artist, blew himself out so that I couldn't possibly tighten the girths, and stood with his ears back and his tail clamped to his rump, looking like a surly, pin-toed brood mare.

The artist was enchanted. "What a beautiful creature," he observed with genuine admiration.

The beautiful creature's nose was corrugated with the effort of holding his breath to ensure that we never got to Wembley. A feinted blow to the stomach let out enough affronted wind to enable me to tweak up the girths and the balance strap, and to scramble onto the slippery saddle in an undignified bustle as a preliminary to being photographed from every possible angle – long shots, short shots, side and back shots, face shots, hand shots, saddlery shots, horse anatomy shots (during which the hack cheered up and became almost animated), tail close–ups, hocks, plaits, ears, nose and throat. There was no end to it.

"And what size," the artist said at last, rising from the winter grass where he had lovingly captured on celluloid the aging tortoiseshell

. . . I ran past it, glancing over my shoulder

hooves, "would Madam like the finished portrait to be?"

"Oh," I said vaguely, not having thought about it, "About three feet square?"

"Gilt-framed, of course?" he said, "with a classical background?"

"Well, naturally."

Some months later, a large, flat parcel arrived by BRS Carriers, supported by two men, plastered with 'Fragile', 'With Care' and similar warnings. Unpacking it, I waded through half a ton of corrugated paper, a set of wooden splints and several large wedges of cardboard. The portrait of a lady, handled with care, was within. Three feet by three feet is very large. It makes, as they say in the world of advertising, for maximum visual impact.

I backed away. I closed my eyes hard, then opened them again. I looked at it close up. I viewed it from afar. I looked at it from the left, I looked at it from the right. I ran past it, glancing over my shoulder. I propped it up in unexpected places so that I could come upon it suddenly, round a corner. It didn't make the slightest difference; whichever way I looked at it, it was horrible.

Encased in a gilt frame of dubious quality was a vast expanse of brackish green. To the right, and hovering slightly, was a draped urn of the type commonly glimpsed in grim city graveyards; and around the base of the urn, a pantomime fog began to curl ominously across the lower half of the canvas. In the midst of this low-slung cloud, a wooden horse stood hock-deep, his glass eyes staring sightlessly out of his stuffed head, carrying upon his back a fine replica of a side-saddle with every buckle standing out in terrible detail. Aloft, roundly upholstered in dead black, sat a giantess, a cobweb stretching from nose to hat brim.

Many years later, when we left our village inn in Hertfordshire, the portrait was left behind as part of the fixtures and fittings. For all I know it might still be there, hung in a dark and beamy corner, gaining a venerable patina of nicotine and spray-polish. It may not be worthy as a memorial to the hack who is long gone, but it does serve a purpose. It is a grim warning to those who would aspire to be immortal. No one, but no one, could deny it.

SHOW BUSINESS

Shows. I've seen them from every angle. In my youth, clad in a spiky, tweed coat, elephant-ear jodhpurs and sensible lace-up shoes, with my hair fiercely plaited and my heart thudding uncomfortably in my chest, shows were the highlight of my life. No matter that I never survived the first two fences in the junior jumping, no matter that in the best pony and rider class I would be propping up the back line, no matter that I was always first out in musical chairs; it was the participation, not the prize, that satisfied. The show was the thing.

I've seen shows as a reporter, when the classes, the prizes and the exhibits paled to insignificance beside other, more vital, considerations. Would the editor swallow my expenses? What would the weather be like? How far from the car park were the horse rings? How far from the horse rings was the bar?

I've even seen shows as a professional, producing not-quite-top-class exhibits from my own tiny yard when, with their owners squinting balefully over the rails and their livery cheques as yet unwritten, it was quite definitely the prize, not the participation, that was the thing.

Far more nerve-racking than any of these though, have been the shows I have seen as a parent. With my pockets full of chalk blocks and vaseline and my lapels bristling with plaiting needles, I have stood helpless at the ringside with sweat beading my brow. I have become short of breath. I have clung onto the ropes with whitened knuckles and ground my teeth. I have felt grey hairs springing through my scalp and wrinkles forming on my face in the time it took to judge a first pony class. This is by no means unusual. Parents who have tiny children in the ring can always be distinguished by their deathly pallor and the way their fingernails are chewed down to the quick. Reminding them that showing is supposed to be fun doesn't help at all.

The following articles are all to do with the perils and frustrations of showing small ponies and children.

A Leading-Rein Lament

I had a small daughter, two hundred pounds and a yen to be back in the show ring. I decided to buy a leading-rein pony. The thought of walking beside an immaculately turned-out pony and child under the eye of a benevolent judge upon the green sward of England's showgrounds fired my imagination. It seemed to me a wonderful idea; the perfect recreation. My friends and their ponies had won all over the country. With their help and experience, how could I fail?

Quite how much things had changed since my own appearance inside the rails was brought home to me sharply when my daughter stood before me in the riding clothiers, decked out in costly, present-day showing regalia. Gone was the itchy tweed, and in its place was a jacket of smooth, blue cloth with a velvet collar, exactly matching the deep-pile, high-crown, velvet, riding cap. Vanished were the ballooning, khaki jodhpurs, replaced by stretchy, lemon ones, fitting with never a wrinkle over the tiny, black, elastic-sided boots with lightweight soles.

Of course, the salesman assured me, the whole effect would be ruined without the trim, collared shirt, the blue, silk tie, and the tiniest, thinnest, leather gloves at three pounds and fifty pence a pair. It was at this point that my daughter began to weep. The showing clothes, it transpired, were not exactly what she had in mind when she had agreed to decorate the show pony; she would have vastly preferred a fairy dress with wings on the back. I paid the bill and as we left the shop, I felt slightly uneasy. I had spent over a quarter of my money and I had only a carrier bag of unwanted clothes to show for it. It was a taste of what was to follow.

It didn't take me long to find what I fondly imagined to be a suitable pony. He was a four-year-old grey gelding, placid by nature and full of pony character. I paid a hundred pounds for him and at the time I thought it was a lot of money. My friends were hysterical when they saw him. "Can't you see," they cried, "that he's lumpy, cresty, long in the back, appley quartered, piggy eyed, that he entirely lacks quality, that both his front legs come out of the same hole, and, what's more," (they added with ill-concealed delight), "he doesn't move straight." I sold him.

My next purchase was another grey. He was a Welsh gelding of Coed Coch breeding, eight years old and twelve hands high. He had bright blue eyes and his name was William. He had a wonderful temperament and my daughter adored him at first sight. He cost me almost three hundred pounds. My friends drifted in and regarded him morosely. "He is a nice enough pony," they finally admitted. "Nice, that is, for child's first or small working hunter pony classes. But of course, he is no use at all for leading-rein. He's too big."

With a sinking heart I pointed out that he was well within the height limit, he had a Life Measurement Certificate to prove it. It was no matter, they said, and plonking my daughter on the pony's snowy back, they proceeded to demonstrate that the pony was not only too big for her, but also too wide. It all boiled down, they said, to suitability.

Eventually I was forced to concede, but when I suggested that we should part with William, my daughter clung fiercely to one of his legs and wept bitterly. I decided to compromise. After all, within the space of a few years, I should possibly be crying out for a child's first or a small working hunter pony. I advertised in the horsy press for a suitable showing family and leased him out for two seasons.

Now there was a problem. I had spent all my money and yet I still had only the carrier bag of unworn clothes in return. It was all rather awkward. I approached my husband for a loan. He was doubtful, but having a generous nature, was soon persuaded. After all, he was aware that I had some previous form behind me. Hadn't I, somewhere in the dim and distant past, been placed third at Richmond? Surely I must know what I was doing.

In the meantime, my friends had decided that as I had made such startling blunders so far, they had better take me in hand. They found me a little Cusop-bred pony which, they enthused, was all that a leading-rein should be with some to spare. I liked the sound of the pony a lot better than I liked the price, which was four hundred pounds.

My friends were loud in their praises. The pony had the sweetest little head imaginable, (it was another gelding), the most wonderful conformation, a floating, extravagant action, and bags of presence (without which, they assured me, he would never be noticed). He was also exactly the right size for the child. Of course, by now I must realise that had I allowed them a free hand earlier, I should have been saved much money and anguish. "Enthusiasm," they said piously, "is no substitute for experience."

Humbly, I agreed and took delivery of the pony with feelings of relief. The feeling was only temporary. The pony was indeed all they had promised and some to spare, but my daughter kept falling off it. He was not naughty, but his movements were quick and darting. His extravagant, floating action dislodged my short-legged daughter at a trot. It obeyed and anticipated her fumbling aids so quickly that she dropped off going round corners. When the pony stopped she flew up his neck. After a while she enjoyed playing with him in the stable but, quite understandably, refused to ride him. All this was almost too much to be endured. I advertised the pony for sale with little hope of getting my money back, his talents seeming somewhat limited. He couldn't be ridden off the leading-rein as apparently a leading-rein show pony was just what its title implied and one could not reasonably expect it to perform otherwise. My friends had warned me never to let go of it. "If you do," they had said, "it will be *off.*" I believed this to be true of mine and all leading-rein ponies and I kept a firm grip on the rein.

Unexpectedly I sold the pony easily and I actually made a profit. I met him many times later in the show ring where he was a great success for his new owners, but he was not the pony for me.

Heartened though, by the sale and the profit margin, I set out again and this time I found a suitable pony. It was a mare. She was eleven hands high and dark bay and my daughter was able to ride her with complete safety both on and off the leading-rein. We loved her and my friends, at first mortally affronted by their rebuff, liked her too.

But having found a suitable pony at last, my problems were by no means over. As everyone hastened to point out, they were only just beginning. The pony was very small and even the smallest of ready-made tack was too big. I had a dainty bridle specially made out of bootlace leatherwork, and after I had covered the browband with red velvet and combed the country for a stainless-steel eggbutt snaffle small enough, it was proclaimed more or less satisfactory.

. . . she dropped off going around corners

The saddle was less easy. I lost count of the number I tried, they were too big, too wide, too new, too shabby; they sat up too high or dropped too low on the withers; they were too long, the flaps were too large, not cut away enough; the bars were not recessed enough. Finally, when the chosen saddle had had its stuffing rearranged by a mystified saddler and a point strap added, everyone hailed it a success, except me – I maintained that it didn't fit the pony – and my daughter, who said it was flat, slippery and uncomfortable.

All that now remained was for me to produce the pony in show-ring condition. If I had imagined for one minute that I was just going to hook it out of the field the day before the show and shampoo it, twiddle a few plaits and clip on a leading-rein, I was sadly mistaken. My friends were there to see that I tackled the job in a professional manner. I was going to do the job the hard way. I was about to discover at first hand how time-consuming and physically exhausting the production of a show animal, albeit a small one, really was.

Just after Christmas, the pony came in from the paddock, was wormed, had her teeth rasped and her feet attended to. She was then rugged up in order that her summer coat would be through in time for the early shows. My idea of rugging up was a jute rug and a blanket. My friends giggled at me indulgently and added two more blankets and the travelling rug out of the back of my car.

They inspected my feed room. The oats were all right, but hardly suitable fodder for a small pony who was to carry an infant. The bran was poor stuff, the hay was moderate, but where was the sugar beet pulp, the whole barley, the linseed? I bought a large polythene container in which to soak fresh sugar beet every day; I ruined my jam kettle boiling quantities of barley and linseed to put condition on the little mare. The whole house reeked. Struggling back with my shopping from the village store, the smell of it met me half way down the lane.

My friends appeared after an interval of a few weeks to see how I was getting on. They stared at the pony in consternation. Couldn't I see it was too fat? Now they came to mention it of course, I could. I began to panic. I restricted its diet and stepped up the exercise. "Don't do that," they cried, "you'll get it too fit and it will lose its manners." I slackened off the exercise and strapped furiously at the layers of fat. The pony began to look muscle-bound. It seemed to have ridges of muscle all over the place. I stopped strapping.

My friends decided that the answer lay in the feeding. "Cut out the hay and feed more solids," said one. "Cut down the solids and feed more hay," advised another. I cut both to meagre and unfair proportions. "It's eating its bedding," they cried, "use shavings." I located a saw mill and filled huge sacks from a hopper twice a week. Sawdust covered my hair, my clothes, filled the car, the house, clogged the hoover, the washing machine and finally, blocked the drains. But the pony returned to its normal size.

Exercise, with my daughter at school and the evenings as yet dark, was another problem. Advice varied from two hours to ten minutes a day, from lungeing to road work to long reins. I worked out my own system. My daughter rode at week ends, following me on my bicycle along the lanes. The pony and I rested on Mondays. On Tuesdays I lunged her for half an hour with side-reins, on Wednesdays I lunged her for half an hour without, but with a saddle instead of a roller. On Thursdays we went out for a walk round the bridle-ways, and on Fridays I rode her myself for a short time in the corner of the paddock where I hoped that no-one could see me – such a ridiculous spectacle I looked on a pony eleven hands high. In between this regime, I toiled and scraped at the old winter coat, picked hairs off my clothes, my carpets and out of my coffee; I mucked out, collected shavings, boiled linseed and barley, soaked sugar beet pulp. My house became unswept and unpolished, my telephone shrilled away unanswered, flowers petrified in their vases.

The early shows loomed frighteningly close. I became nervous. I practised plaiting the mare's newly pulled mane and in my agitation cut out half a plait. My friends decided that I had better have a dress rehearsal. I was to prepare the pony as for a show and they would act as judges.

The day of the dress rehearsal came; my friends arrived for the inspection. On my side, our friendship was wearing thin. I was an exhausted nervous wreck. I told myself that if they found any fault with my production whatsoever, it would be the end, the absolute finish, of cordial relations. They did, of course, the list was endless.

I hadn't trimmed the whiskers off the end of her nose, I hadn't cleaned out her ears with the clippers. I hadn't pulled the mane enough at the crest so that although my plaits started off at the withers like neat little marbles, by the time they got half way up they were like golf balls. My tail-pulling was messy, I hadn't put vaseline round eyes, nose and dock. I had forgotten the hoof oil. I hadn't chalked her white sock. The saddle was too far forward. The child needed a tiny button-hole, and was I seriously intending to go into the ring in those clothes? I was not smart enough. What I needed was a navy trouser suit. How could I expect to compete with bowler-hatted men in dark suits with red carnations in their lapels?

The criticism mounted. The pony's coat did not shine as much as it should; perhaps the shavings were making it dusty. I must keep a spotless cotton sheet on under the blankets and make a linen hood with which to cover up the pony the night before a show. More strapping was needed, and a final polish with a damp cloth would remove any surface dust. I must remember to provide a supply of navy tape with which to replace the yards of cheap, white string dished out at the show with the numbers. The white leading-rein was not quite right after all, with the pony having a white blaze down its face, a plain, leather one would be more tasteful. The child looked very nice, but a little grave, couldn't she manage to look as if she was enjoying it?

I sighed and set to work on the dust sheets for the pony. I had come this far and I couldn't give up now. I hunted out a pair of good linen sheets and, using another friend's hood as a pattern, I cut out a smaller one for the mare. Piles of domestic mending, untouched since the previous December, were thrown to one side as I machined away furiously, making eye holes, ear holes, and stitching on tapes.

The problem of transport reared its ugly head. Nervously I approached my husband. The thought of having a trailer attached to his car filled him with almost as much horror as having to buy one. No, he said finally, if I wanted a trailer, I must sell my own Mini and buy a larger vehicle, capable of pulling my own trailer. I could hardly argue. I exchanged my Mini for an ancient but worthy Rover. I tracked down a suitable trailer which cost me over two hundred pounds; a tow bar added another twenty. The new car had an insatiable appetite for petrol. I no longer dared to calculate how much 'the perfect recreation' had cost, but I knew that I had started out with two hundred pounds and had spent over two thousand. I tried to tell myself that the worst was now over, that the fun was just about to begin. Yet when I thought about the first show, creeping inexorably nearer, I got the most terrible stage-fright. I was terrified. I felt really ill.

It passed, that first show, in a haze of panic. When the alarm clock rang to summon us to the stable in the middle of the previous night, it was already raining hard. I was very tempted to roll over and forget it. Husband and daughter though, were not to be put off. Six long, arduous months they had waited for this day and they were not going to allow me to back out at the last moment. I plaited by torchlight with numbed fingers and listened to the rain beating on the stable roof. Through the downpour we drove the Rover and its trailer to the showground. We bought a catalogue at the gate.

There were twelve ponies entered in the leading-rein class, but, owing to the weather, when the commentator called them into the ring, there were only three forward. I don't remember much about the judging apart from the cold, my nerves, and the sheer soaking discomfort of it all. I know that rain dribbled off my daughter's hat and the pony's nose, and that the navy trouser suit finished the day two inches shorter than it had started out. Oddly, my daughter enjoyed herself, the pony enjoyed it too, and even my husband enjoyed watching from the sanctuary of the car. It was only me, who felt wretched.

When the judging was over we stood third, or last, whichever way you like to look at it. The chief steward paddled along to remind us that we must stay for the grand parade at four o'clock or lose our prize money. The time was nine twenty-five am.

We sat all day in the Rover, occasionally making a foray into the hedge bottoms to pull grass for the pony. Having no knowledge of grand parades, we had not brought enough food for her. Neither for ourselves. About lunch-time we struggled along duck boards laid along the dripping avenues of trade stands in order to consume damp ham sandwiches in the refreshment tent. One of my friends spotted us and came over in order to congratulate us upon the sodden yellow rosette hooked into my proud daughter's top pocket.

"Of course," she said conversationally, "what you really need is a proper little horse box with some living accomodation in it, then the weather wouldn't really bother you quite so much."

My husband dropped his carton of tea. My daughter's eyes grew wide with anticipation. My purse, my current account, and my post office savings book were empty, but my nerves had gone, the sky was brightening, and later I would lead my pony and my daughter in the grand parade. A 'proper little horse box' sounded just what I needed.

A Tale of Two Fishes

The highlight of the season was the day we were presented with a British Show Pony Society perpetual challenge cup. It was quite splendid, being fifteen inches high with a black plinth and curly handles. It was also hallmarked silver. It would have looked very nice on the sideboard. I say *would have* because having presented us with it, the judge took it back and there followed a chain of events, the result of which was that we only saw it again twice, each time for about thirty seconds.

The winning of the cup was a fluke, or so the other exhibitors intimated at the time, but we were delighted. Even my husband who, the previous week, had loudly and publicly declared that he was having no further connection with our showing activities, not ever, cheered up considerably as he pocketed the prize money and drifted craftily towards the bar. Flushed with triumph, I led the pony back to the trailer, dispatching small daughter in the direction of the secretary's tent to collect the cup. When I had bandaged, rugged, watered and fed the pony and she still hadn't returned, I got rather worried.

I found her still at the secretary's tent, weeping copiously over a pile of numbers and being regarded with alarm by several official personages. The secretary herself greeted me with exclamations of much relief. "I have been trying to explain to her that she cannot have the cup today," she said. "It is Our Policy to retain the cup for engraving and to post it on to the winner within ten days."

I could see that this was reasonable, but small daughter was in despair. Not being able to bear the trophy home in glory after we had won it was the end of the world.

"I don't suppose I could take it and have it engraved myself?" I suggested.

The secretary and the official personages threw up their hands in horror at the thought of it. "Engrave it yourself!" they cried in outraged tones. "A Perpetual Challenge Cup belonging to the British Show Pony Society! Whoever heard of such a thing! Besides," they added, "it is against Our Policy."

I ushered small daughter out of the tent feeling that I had perhaps made an improper suggestion. I felt they suspected I was the kind of person who would scratch my name on their precious trophy with a pin.

In order to console ourselves we visited the amusement stalls at the far end of the showground. I purchased five ping-pong balls for small daughter to throw at a regiment of jam jars.

"Don't imagine that you are going to keep goldfish," my husband warned. "Nasty, smelly things."

"She won't win anything," I said reassuringly, just as one ball settled into a jar, closely followed by another. It was obviously our day for flukes. The attendant presented Emma with two little plastic bags of water, each containing a goldfish. My husband regarded them with distaste. They travelled home in the water bucket.

My husband, inveterate goldfish hater, went out again as soon as we got home and returned with a glass bowl, a drum of fish food, a packet of gravel, some shells, a small mermaid, and some things in a bag of water that he said were live water fleas. He had spent almost all of the prize money by now, and he lovingly fed the fish every day. I was not fond of them. Our dogs regarded them with anticipation. Small daughter was not wild about them either.

We waited patiently for the perpetual challenge cup to arrive. After about a month, during which small daughter had watched for the postman every day, I rang the show secretary. She was apologetic but vague. The delay was regrettable but the jewellers were exceedingly busy. Doubtless the cup would be arriving within the next few days. I let another month go by before I rang again with much the same result.

Friends drifted in and out as they do during the summer. Those of the showing variety always managing to end up in the tack room, which enabled them to count our rosettes and let slip how very many more they had at home.

"Not won a BSPS cup this year then?" they would remark, looking pointedly at the scattered trophies on the side-board.

"Oh yes," I would reply, "we won one in May but it hasn't arrived yet."

"Fancy," they would say, accompanied by a nudge and a wink. "Won one in May and it hasn't arrived yet."

Clearly I was disbelieved.

In July I became agitated. In August I became angry. In September I took action. I wrote to the British Show Pony Society and complained vociferously.

Now I have never had any cause for complaint against the BSPS. Throughout my showing years I found them an entirely helpful and worthy organisation and so efficacious was the letter immediately despatched from the secretary of the BSPS to the secretary of the show concerned, that the following day the cup arrived.

Its arrival brightened the day somewhat because the previous day there had been a catastrophe. One of the fish had died. In case it had died of something infectious, my husband had rushed out and purchased something called 'Antiseptifish' which had turned the water bright yellow. He watched the remaining fish with much anxiety.

We unpacked the perpetual challenge cup with reverence and set it in the midst of the breakfast table. Small daughter regarded it with delight. I looked at it carefully. My husband regarded it thunderously. I rang the show secretary.

"The cup is not engraved," I said.

"Not engraved?" she repeated in the tones of the very greatest astonishment. "Not *engraved*?"

"Not engraved," I said. "For five long months we have been waiting for someone to engrave ten words upon it. They are not there."

"Then you must return the cup to the jeweller at once," she commanded. "We don't allow the winners to hold the cup until the engraving is done. It is against Our Policy."

I replaced the receiver and there followed a prolonged and woeful discussion with the BSPS. They agreed that it was the most awful shame. "We can get it engraved for you," they said comfortingly, "but it will take a little time and you would have to pay the postage. In all respects and after all you have endured, it might be preferable to take it to your local jeweller and get it engraved yourself."

We did.

Our local jeweller doesn't do his own engraving; he had to send it away to be done. There was a postal strike. On the day we collected the cup with the ten words faithfully engraved upon it, we also had a card from the show secretary.

Would you please return the British Show Pony Society's perpetual challenge trophy, she said, as its early return was essential to the smooth running of the forthcoming show.

Not Quite a First Pony

On the way to Brailes Show, the wheels fell off the Trimbee trailer. The Trimbees, after having reassured themselves that the pony within was unscathed, stood in the road and regarded the wreckage with dismay but without surprise, because all things considered, it was a miracle it had held together at all.

Travelling in convoy as we were, it was a while before I realised that my wing mirror was empty. It was only after much anxious deliberation and some heart-rending reversing in an inconvenient gateway, that I eventually retraced my route along the road and arrived at the scene of the breakup. It was all most annoying as naturally, we were already behind schedule and ours were the first classes of the day. Panic-stricken consultations resulted in Olly Trimbee, resplendent in lemon and navy, and Mrs Trimbee clambering into the car beside me, leaving poor Mr Trimbee at the roadside with the pony, to hitch a lift to the show-ground as best he might.

When we arrived at the show, the rosettes for the leading-rein class were just being handed out, and the commentator was calling insistently for the first ridden ponies. As the Trimbee's first ridden pony was still hitching its way to the show, and our leading-rein pony had missed its class, both jockeys burst into tears.

Experienced showing people will immediately recognise all this as a perfectly normal turn of events; a commonplace, a run of the mill affair in a sport (and I use the word in the loosest possible sense) beset by so many frustrations and difficulties that the bad days outnumber the good ones by ten to one.

But wait, there is more. Out of two possible combinations we could salvage but one, and with stoic determination born of many similar occasions, we hoisted Olly Trimbee, jockey of the absent first ridden pony onto the present leading-rein pony, let down the safety stirrups and ushered the pair into the ring. Typically, the jockey would have to jib at the last minute. With the tears of recent outrage as yet undried upon her cheeks she faced us across the ropes. "I can't remember what to do," she wailed, "I don't think I can manage."

Mrs Trimbee, assuming the authority of a hard-boiled showing parent, reassured the child with an airy wave of the hand. "Just follow everyone else round and do what they do and you will be perfectly all right." Olly Trimbee blew her nose and rode on into the class, looking troubled; as well she might, the little bay never before having set foot into a show-ring in its life other than attached to a leading-rein.

With no pre-ring preparation to take off her sparkle, the little bay performed magnificently when she was following the others. She bent her little neck and pricked her ears. Olly grew more confident and her plaits bobbed up and down and we at the ropes clasped our hands in delight; then the judge called Olly in first. Far from being a triumph, this was a disaster because with nobody to watch and 'do what they do', and nobody to follow, Olly and the little bay pony were sunk. We at the ringside began to make signs to the pair at the top of the line. With our hands and our arms we described circles to be trotted and figure eights to be cantered and all to no avail. Olly's face grew pale and registered only incomprehension. In no time at all the judge was inviting her to perform.

With the eyes of the ringside upon her, Olly squeezed the pony with her legs. Nothing happened. The little bay stood stoutly in line, having learned at an early age never to move an inch in the show ring without an attendant. Olly's squeezes became kicks and the hue of her face changed from white to pink, but the little bay still refused to proceed alone. The chief steward tried to help by making encouraging clicking noises and flapping his arms but still nothing happened.

. . . I clung to the ropes

Finally, Olly lost all patience, raised her leather-covered cane and gave the little bay a thwack which reverberated around the show-ground. Having never before experienced chastisement from above (leading-rein riders are not allowed to carry sticks), the little bay shot out of line like a cork out of a champagne bottle and proceeded to fly in demented circles like a half blown up balloon that somebody had loosed by mistake. Round and round she flew as I clung to the ropes like a drowning soul and Mrs Trimbee covered her eyes and other showing people strolled up to us and said, "Is that your little bay pony in the ring?" as people will when things start to get out of control.

The St. John's Ambulance Brigade had been alerted and were standing by with a stretcher by the time the little bay spotted a solid and solitary figure in a felt hat and decided that this must certainly be the attendant she had mislaid. The pony made a thankful dive for the judge, Miss Sybil Smith, Royal Riding Mistress, and skidded to a halt an inch away from her shoelaces, shooting Olly straight up her neck. Miss Sybil Smith didn't even flinch. As Olly wriggled her way back down the pony's plaits, she simply wagged an admonitory finger at pony and child. "I don't think you two have ever been off the leading-rein before," she said sternly, "and I don't think you had better do it again."

Mr Trimbee, who had managed to thumb down a large horse box carrying show jumpers, arrived in the nick of time to see the pair being dispatched in disgrace to the bottom of the line.

To add insult to injury, when the Trimbees went back for their trailer a week later, only the wheels remained. The rest of it could be clearly discerned in a nearby field, being utilised as a henhouse.

A Transport of No Delight

To be perfectly honest, we didn't need a horse box. Our trailer had been entirely reliable, smooth-running and economical. We had been perfectly satisfied with it. The purchase of the horse box was sheer folly. Nevertheless, purchased it was.

The first thing I noticed about the new horse box was that it was too wide to go through the gate into the yard. My husband, our neighbour and a passing cyclist spent almost half an hour trying. The lane rang with, "Left hand down a bit," "Come on a bit," "Hold it there now – whoa!" and similar cries peculiar to such manoeuvres. In the end they gave up and left it parked in the lane, causing a major traffic hazard for the village.

After some fruitless telephone calls we found a local farmer who said most certainly, delighted to have the horse box standing under his old barn, providing we paid two pounds a week rent. We paid. It was quite a walk whenever we wanted to put something into the horse box or simply to admire it. We tried not to think about the trailer, that it had passed through the yard gate easily, with inches to spare on either side.

As a matter of fact, ours was a very nice horse box. It had room for two horses, it had compartments for tack and tools and fodder and, best of all, it had living accomodation; a double and a single bunk, a sink, a cooker and a fridge. My husband, who had never in his life even been inside a caravan, was highly diverted by all this. In the first week he broke the water heater, nearly blew himself up by buying the wrong sort of gas, lost the sink plug, cut his hand on the glass shade of the gas light and crushed the mantle.

Our friends arrived at intervals to view this latest extravaganza. "Bit big, isn't it?" they said. "Bit daft having all that space just for one little pony. Would have thought the transit would have suited you better."

"What's a transit?" we said, interested.

"It's smaller, and it's under three tons," they said. "Yours isn't, but of course, you've got your HGV licence."

"Our what?" we asked.

My husband spent the next four weekends driving round a disused airfield, reversing in and out of little piles of rubble whilst I pretended to be traffic lights. He passed the test. We stuck up the certificate in the cab of the horse box. My husband stuck up a postcard beside it which said, "I am now awaiting my next (dis)appointment." It wasn't long in coming.

Our next visitor walked round the box one way, then the other, staring at the sides. "Where's the personnel door?" she said eventually.

I replied that there wasn't one. Having walked round the box three or four times, surely she could see that.

"How will you keep an eye on the pony when you are driving along?" she wanted to know. "How will you check that it hasn't got a foot in its hay net, or been stung by a bee, or similar awful fate?"

Rather annoyed by the voicing of such alarmist notions, I retorted that I wouldn't know until I let down the ramp, pointing out that the same limitation had applied to the trailer, and no awful fates had occurred so far.

"Ah, well!" she said triumphantly. "A trailer is a trailer. A horse box is a different kettle of fish altogether."

With which I was forced to agree.

The following visitor admitted that the horse box was a very fine-looking vehicle.

"Mechanically perfect," my husband boasted, patting the bonnet fondly.

"They have to be these days," our visitor agreed, "to get through the plating."

"To get through the what?" we said.

We booked the horse box into the nearest vehicle testing centre. It was thirty miles away. My husband took a day off work to attend. It failed. When he got home he looked rather pale. He took the report sheet along to the local garage and told them to put everything right. The bill came to two hundred and sixty-eight pounds. We tried not to think of the trailer, ousted by the aluminium, money-gobbling extravaganza. Next time, the horse box passed the plating.

The showing season was almost upon us. We decided to make a stupendous effort and go to the first big early show. We had never been before. It was usually too far, and too early for us. I couldn't wait for everyone to see us roll up in our new horse box. I imagined their mouths falling open with astonishment. Some might even faint with envy. Perhaps the sight of such splendour would have such a demoralising effect upon the opposition that we would win our class on the strength of it.

We made up our minds to travel the day before our class in order to really enjoy ourselves and to gain the full benefit of the living accomodation. When I opened the tool compartment to put my pitchfork and brush inside, I discovered that it was packed with crates of beer.

My husband was lying on his back poking lighted spills underneath the fridge. "Damn the thing," he said. "If I can't get it to light now, I shall have no ice for tomorrow."

My heart sank as I stowed my tools into the fodder compartment; the next thing we should need was a licence to serve alcoholic refreshment. By mid-afternoon the fridge was lit, the pony was loaded, our daughter was installed in the cab, we were ready to start out. My husband looked round anxiously. Had we remembered everything? The saddlery? The milk? The maps? The hay nets? The bottle opener?

He pulled out the choke and turned the key in the ignition. There was a long dismal groan, a cough, then silence. The procedure was repeated several times towards the end of which there was not even a groan or a cough. The horse box refused to start.

Alone of the three, I remained calm and resigned. Small daughter wept. My husband grew very red about the neck and lost his temper.

Eventually he flung himself out of the cab, leapt into his car and drove like a madman down to the local garage. The mechanic who returned hard on his heels diagnosed a flat battery. After a lot of fiddling under the bonnet and under the passenger seat with jump leads they got us started. The mechanic assured us that the journey would recharge the battery.

"Big horse boxes," he said severely, "are not meant to sit under barns for four months at a time; they need using."

Driving along was very nice, but when we had been going for about two hours my husband began to mutter that he was not sure he was on the right road. It might be advisable for me to consult the map. My husband's idea of a map is a world atlas measuring two feet by one foot and weighing about five pounds. The first page I opened it at showed the north face of the moon.

It took us quite a while to get back on the right road. When we reached the showground, the events of the day were over. And naturally, as our classes were not until the next day, none of our friends were there to greet us. There was nobody to faint with envy at our superb luxury horse box, mechanically perfect.

We stabled and fed the pony and climbed thankfully into the living accommodation. Sugar crunched beneath our feet. The sliding cupboards had done just that during the journey. All our provisions and crockery were strewn across the floor. We rescued what we could.

We washed in cold water. Naturally, the water heater wasn't working. It was comforting though, to know that there was plenty of ice in the fridge.

I cooked a makeshift meal on the cooker. Cooking smells gathered in the living accommodation. It grew very hot. Every time we opened the door or a window the gas went out. After the meal we washed up. It was hard to shift the grease from the plates with cold water. We couldn't fill the sink from the kettle because we didn't have a plug. My husband sat on the edge of his bunk looking grey-faced and totally exhausted. Clutched to his chest was a blue plastic beaker containing whisky and an enormous chunk of ice. "Know what I'm going to do tomorrow?" he said.

I shook my head, remembering with some misgiving, the contents of the tool compartment.

"I'm going to find someone who buys horseboxes," he said.

Hell is a County Show

Yesterday we won our first major prize. I wouldn't want to live through it again for a thousand pounds. The show was in the South of England, which entailed driving there the day before and staying overnight. Contrary to what our friends told us, living in the horse box is not comfortable. It is not congenial. It is HELL. Even now, in high summer, when in the daytime the living accommodation is like a roaring furnace, at nights it is *cold*. We lay frozen in our bunks, sniffing the air anxiously lest the Calor Gas be leaking and we were all discovered in the morning, poisoned as we slept. About midnight a troublesome animal in the temporary stabling began to kick the boards; he finally settled down as dawn illuminated the skylight, by which time, if I had had a gun, I would have cheerfully shot it clean between the eyes, regardless of the consequences.

As it seemed to be light I got up. The walls were pouring with condensation. My clothes felt damp. I made my way across the deserted showground to the public lavatories. They were not a pretty sight. A heavy dew soaked through my shoes into my socks. I went to look at the pony.

The pony was in the pink. In comparison with ours, hers was luxury, five-star accommodation. She had a warm, timber stable, comfortably bedded down with straw (which she is not allowed at home because she eats it) and beneath that, as she had already discovered, if she scraped hard enough, she came to grass. She had regular meals, fresh water, lots of visitors, and could chat to her neighbours over the half door. Squelching my way back to the horse box I reflected that if anyone asked which were the dumb animals, you couldn't, in all honesty, say it was the equines.

The showground was laid out with a wonderful disregard for convenience. About three miles from the horse box park, the show committee had provided an undefined exercising area for ponies in a never-never land sandwiched between the show-jumpers crashing backwards and forwards over practice poles, and colossal heavyweight hunters thundering to and fro improving their gallop. Small daughter, now graduated to the first pony class, and taking her first faltering and uncertain steps without an attendant, gamely struggled to perfect her individual display, fleeing for her life on every second loop and being bumped into by stray members of the public who, their eyes fixed purposefully upon the scarlet coats of the show-jumpers, hoped to catch a glimpse of somebody they recognised from the television.

The class was judged in the main ring at noon. The showground was packed solid with people determined to get their money's worth and have a good time if they died in the effort.

It took half an hour to get through the crowd who stood twenty deep at the rails of the main ring whose flag poles were all we could see to distinguish it. The heat and the crush and the agonisingly slow progress through the melee were frightening. I grew panic-stricken about the baby in the push-chair pushed up against the pony's hind legs and failed to notice that she had stretched out her nose and taken an ice-cream from a child in front. At one point we were completely swallowed up by the crowd and lost sight of even the flags. People wouldn't, or couldn't let us through. We didn't command the respect of the lumbering shires with their shaved tails and their soup-plate hooves, or the brewery drays, clanking along with more iron-mongery than the QE2. So I used my elbows, the pony butted people in the small of their backs with her nose and small daughter shrilled, "Excuse us, excuse us, *please*," as we laboured along, sickened by the smell of frying doughnuts and sweat, bumping into giant inflated balloon merchants without permits, tripping over the cables for the vibratory massage, and eventually arrived at the main ring only to be shooed away by a perspiring steward, "You can't come in here, this is the exit; the entrance is over the other side, through the fun fair."

Having gained the comparative sanctuary of the ring at last, our pony won the class because, to judge by the size of its stomach, it had been awake all night eating its bedding and was now too tired and too bloated to misbehave. The other first ponies, appalled by the hustle, the heat, the bandstand, and the way the crowd clapped them enthusiastically every time they passed the grandstand, scooted round the ring with their eyes starting out of their heads and their tiny riders hauling uselessly at the reins.

The grand parade was at four o'clock and obligatory for all prize-winners. From the four corners of the show ground, slow processions of cattle, heavy horses, goats, driving turn-outs, hunters, mares and foals, young stock and coster's carts could be seen making their way towards the main ring. It was murder. To aggravate matters, having had every separate toe trodden into the sod and been

. . . hoping to catch a glimpse of somebody from television

bumped, jostled and crushed from every angle in order to convey pony and infant to the centre of the proceedings, nobody seemed to want us when we arrived. The parade was a shambles.

The high spot of the event was when the chief steward hastened across to ask us if we would mind standing perfectly still because the bull was loose when even I, with my limited knowledge of bovine anatomy, could see that it was only a heifer.

Interminable spirals of livestock in headcollars decorated with rosettes dragged along by red-faced attendants in white coats wound their way into the ring, whilst more than could possibly be accommodated piled up at the entrance. The winner of the leading-rein class was despatched to stand beside us. The pony was already patched with sweat and dancing with agitation, having been almost mown down by a coach and four. The immaculate little child on the pony had both eyes tightly shut and clung grimly to the pommel of the saddle.

Eventually the chief steward found a place for us to join in the procession, waving a hand towards the far end of the arena. We were to follow on after the YFC decorated floats. The leading-rein attendant and I took one look at the last float which, decorated with balloons and streamers, had a pop group on board and left the ring by the President's private entrance, unhooking a ceremonial red rope and crossing his hallowed frontage to do so.

We were boxed up and out of the main gates within ten minutes, but the leading-rein people were still on the road ahead of us. When the grand parade was over, there must have been two solitary, uncollected cups on the trestle tables in front of the grandstand. Quite possibly nobody even wondered why.

The Retirement of Mrs Akrill

Today I decided to retire from the show ring (which will, I tell myself, be its loss, not mine). It is no hasty decision. It is final, pre-meditated, irrevocable.

When I awake I cannot face the prospect of washing and plaiting ponies in a high wind. I am done with pierced fingers and sodden feet, with stretch jodhpurs steaming on the radiators, whitening all over the formica, last week's ice-cream stains on the Wetherill jacket and dirty bits in the sink. I make myself a pot of tea and, over this, I make my decision – today will see the metamorphosis of Mrs Akrill from exhibitor to spectator. The sheer good sense of the decision pleases me. I feed the ponies in an aura of good will. They are faintly surprised when I do not exclaim in horror over the dirty, yellow patches which they have cleverly applied to themselves during the night.

I inform the household of my plans over breakfast. Small daughter, to whom the weekend showing scramble has become something to endure with protests and wailings, weeps into her corn flakes. I am untouched by this fickle demonstration. I remind her that only last Saturday she had implored me to give up showing so that she could take ballet lessons instead. The wails increase in volume.

Eventually, I set forth in joyful anticipation of the day ahead. Armed with the car sticker which is all I have to show for my five pounds entry fee (which I may under no circumstances reclaim), I am dressed in a smart, pleated skirt, navy tights and my good, navy, patent shoes decorated with a gilt stirrup. It makes a nice change from the navy trouser suit whose good cloth is the worse for vaseline, chalk and ponies whose mouths drip green froth.

With no trailer to impede my progress I enjoy the drive to the show. I have a packed lunch. I intend to stroll around the show ground at my leisure. I will watch the classes I choose to see from the grandstand. I will not, however, gain admittance to the show ground without my pony. I display my exhibitor's car sticker to the gateman, who directs me to the exhibitor's entrance, whose attendant refuses me admission on the grounds that I have not brought any livestock with me. Indignantly I wave my exhibitor's badge and cry that my entry has cost me five pounds. The attendant waxes sympathetic, agrees that it is a shame and sends me back to the main entrance where I am forced to pay two pounds to get in, which seems preferable to going home again.

The car park attendant personally conducts me to the farthest and most inconvenient space in the car park, and, when I have gathered my mackintosh (it looks like rain), my lunch (car park too far away to walk back for it), my shooting stick, handbag and other miscellaneous objects, he has the nerve to ask me if I would mind moving my car back six inches to clear the string with which he has marked the parking line. I cry that I would mind very much indeed. I wave my stick threateningly as I hurry off in the direction of the show which I can discern in the far distance. I am annoyed, irritated. I tell myself to relax, that I have just had a bad start, that things will improve.

Today, because I make for the remotest, draughtiest little ring on the ground, which more often than not is the lot of the leading-rein class, and perch upon my stick to consult my catalogue, I discover that the class, unbelievably, is being judged in the main ring. I fold up my stick, gather up my possessions and trek through the avenues of trade stands back to the main arena. Due to my already heavy expenditure I decide against the grandstand. I open my shooting stick amongst a scattering of spectators, rearrange my belongings, and settle in.

The loudspeaker (under which I have unfortunately settled) gives a fair impression of a thunderstorm and announces that the class will begin ten minutes later than advertised. I am not upset. I am almost happy as I enjoy a brief moment of sunshine. I picture the scene in the exhibitors' park; the frantic searching for lost bowlers, sticks, gloves and leading-reins, the last-minute fussing over the ponies; rubbing oil on their faces, chalking their socks, applying polish to their hooves, tweaking out hairs from between their plaits; the parents brushing down their offspring, tying hair-ribbons and numbers, cramming on their hats and buffing up their boots. Threatening. Cajoling. Quentin says he doesn't want to ride and Fenella wants to go to the loo.

How delightful it is, I decide, to be a *spectator*. I feel superior, civilised. The loudspeaker suddenly begins to bark like a dog which is rather aggravating. I wonder if I should move.

Soon, however, I see ponies filtering into the collecting ring. There are only one or two but I am not taken in. Beware the complacent exhibitor who imagines that there are only three in the class and smiles at the thought of the yellow rosette. At the summons of the ring steward, leading-rein ponies can appear out of thin air, suitcases and holes in the ground. And sure enough, here they come. A flash of a blancoed leading-rein, a swish of a silken tail, plaited like children on the first day of school.

Of course, I know them all, but I see them anew from this side of the ropes. I mark those present in my catalogue, which is about the size of a small telephone directory and has a nasty habit of closing itself when I am not looking.

The loudspeaker crackles back into life to the dismay of the nearest pony who takes off like a rocket, almost removing its attendant's arm from its socket. Happily, the judge has only just arrived and is otherwise occupied in the centre of the ring. From my position at the rails I hear all the frantic instructions hissed out from between wooden lips that would be the envy of any ventriloquist: "Shorten your *reins*, Henry," "Sit *up*, Victoria!" "Pull him back a bit, Katie," "Push him on a bit, Horatio!"

As the ponies mince along, the judge surveys each one. I feel some of the reflected pain as each exhibit mechanically puts its ears back or trips over a clump of grass as the judge looks it over, and immediately regains its beauty and presence as soon as she turns her back.

I begin to make little comments at the side of each exhibit named in my catalogue. After all, with my experience I am discerning, knowledgeable. I have not noticed the clouds gathering above my head. The next thunderclap does not come from the loudspeaker. I leap to my feet and gather up my belongings yet again. Hauling on my mackintosh, I head for the grandstand. The raindrops are large and very cold, the attendant asks if I am a member. I admit that I am not. I do not complain about my lost entry fee. I pay another one pound and twenty pence which takes a long time because the attendant is very short of change which he blames onto the show committee, the decimal system and the Common Market.

In the grandstand, I unknowingly choose to sit beside a female version of Al Read. As the ponies go by she gives a commentary, "Nice pony – should be too for the price he paid for it . . . There goes

old So-and-So, he'll be all right today, he lives next door to the judge
. . . Here's old Whatsit, twenty-eight years old if it's a day!''

I look round to see if I can escape but the grandstand has filled up.
The ponies are pulled into line by a steward in preliminary order. I
dare not open my catalogue in case Al Read sees the comments I have
written in it. Now she informs her companion that the pony at the
top of the line has an injection before every show, "You've only got
to look at its eyes to see it's drugged." Next I learn that the pony in
third place is the Demon King itself in the stable and has its food
thrown in over the stable door, and that the secret of another pony's
perfect manners is that its owner arrives at the show the day before
the class and lunges it all night.

Knowing perfectly well that all this is totally without foundation, I
debate whether to shriek with hysterical laughter at each fresh
revelation, or to administer a sound crack at the woman with my
shooting stick, but I am disloyal and cowardly and I do neither.

I now discover that the beautiful head carriage of a bay pony is due
to its being attached to a very heavy weight. "That pony never comes
up for a breath." And that the extravagant floating action of another
was "All done with bamboo canes". The final winner did not escape
either: "That child looks very big for seven, very big indeed. You've
only got to look at the size of its feet to know that it's over age!"

My self control leaves me feeling exhausted and very thirsty. I
leave the grandstand and eventually discover a tea bar. The assistant
snappishly asks me if I haven't anything less than the pound note I
offer. "I have not," I say, "owing to the decimal system and the
Common Market." The assistant sees that I am on her side and
warms to me at once. Soon I am feeling better, revived by the hot,
weak tea, hastily consumed from its rapidly disintegrating container.

Once again I feel invigorated, glad of my decision to retire from the
show ring. I think of the post-mortems taking place in the exhibitors'
park. The winners flushed with victory. The losers sulking and
muttering behind the horse boxes. "I will have none of it," I cry, and
the tea bar assistant nods vigorously in agreement. I deposit my paper
cup in the receptacle provided and decide that I must find another
hobby with which to replace the one so recently and sensibly

abandoned. With this in mind I am ready to appreciate all that the show has to offer.

Inspired by the pleasure horse class I wonder if I should take up riding western style. The idea of wearing a stetson has a certain appeal, but the vertical position of the stirrup leathers is rather worrying and I am not sure that the wooden saddle will be comfortable. The glamour of the ladies' hunter class may be more my style. Perhaps I will learn to ride side-saddle and, veiled and mysterious, ride to hounds. The dashing Mrs Akrill, toast of the shires. Then again, the private driving class is worth consideration. I see myself wearing a smart hat with a feather, my lower limbs encased in a rug, becoming an expert whip. Mrs Akrill driving Hero and Hercules to a Skeleton Brake.

As I stroll along avenue 'C' at the end of the day, force of habit causes me to pause at a saddlery stand. The obliging assistant produces a stetson for me to try. It has a fringe all round the edge and, invited to look into a cheval mirror, I see that I could be mistaken for a standard lamp. The price of the suede-seated side-saddle takes my breath away. Even the holly driving whip with the silver bands is beyond my reach, but on the way out I see a very nice, leather, leading-rein with a stainless steel clip . . .

Nightfall at Newark

Showing the yearling should have been a piece of cake. The yearling had never been any trouble to anybody. There was to be only him and me. No husband, no small daughter, nobody else to consider at all. There was no earthly reason why it should have taken me seven hours to muck out the horse box, wash the yearling's tail, collect his equipment, put on his travelling gear, load him up, and climb into the driver's seat. Yet it did, and the result of this was that it was eight o'clock and dusk when I started out, instead of being just after lunch with the whole afternoon in front of me, as I had planned it.

When I arrived at Newark it was nearly midnight. The show-ground was very silent, very dark. There was no-one at the gate to direct me. The first thing I did was to turn right instead of left at the entrance which took me into the cattle lines. It took an eighteen-point turn accompanied by much anxious mooing from the dairy short-horn tent to get out again.

Safely parked in the horse section at last, and hopefully clutching my stable allocation label, I jumped down from the cab and set off trustingly to find my temporary loose box by the light of a fading bicycle lamp. It was laughable really because as every Newark habitué knows, by Friday, the other exhibitors have swopped, borrowed or removed all the stable numbers and nobody can find anything.

The stable manager's shed was empty and shuttered. There was not a soul to be seen. I wandered up and down the rows of stabling looking for numbers. There weren't any. Eventually, on my third circuit of shuffling along under the sacking which serves as a top door, shining my lamp at sleeping hummocks within and occasion-ally colliding with a sleepless equine head, I found what I imagined to be an empty stable. A bale of straw had been left outside for bedding. I heaved a mighty sigh of relief, opened the lower door and threw it inside. A scream of anguish came from within. I fled.

I trailed back towards the horse box, facing up to the fact that I should have to remove the partition, bed the yearling down in the back, and sleep across the front seats in the cab, curled round the gear-stick which separated them. I was just passing the only lighted horse box in the lines when the personnel door flew open and a body hurtled out clutching a bottle. I recognised the familiar features of a well-known show jumper but he seemed in no fit state to be of any help. I tried anyway. "I can't find my stable," I told him, "I've got my ticket but I can't see the numbers and I've been walking round for ages."

The well-known show jumper lay on the ground with his arms and legs spread out like starfish. He didn't reply.

Several inebriated faces regarded me sympathetically from inside the horse box. "You can schleep in here, if you like," one of them said

. . . the yearling was bedded down in the police kitchen

in an unsteady voice, "provided you don't schnore."

"It isn't for me," I said hastily. "It's for my yearling."

"No yearlings sleeping with me!" shouted the body on the grass, suddenly regaining his faculty for speech.

One of the faces clambered carefully down from the horse box and took me by the elbow. "I know where there's an empty stable," he said. "Just you come with me." Another of the faces wobbled after us. The empty stable was at the end of a row situated a little way from the main block. The show jumpers were wonderfully kind. They found a bale of straw and bedded it down for the yearling. They filled my water bucket at the taps, weaving their way back with it filled to the brim. They fumbled with bandages and tail guards and strung up the hay net. They refused to let me help at all. Fatigued as I was, I stood outside and let them get on with it. There was a lot of ssshing and alcoholic chuckling. The next morning I could see why.

Struggling along the stable block with corn and day rugs and grooming kit, I could see that all the other stables were occupied by the most enormous, immaculate horses. There were a lot of uniforms and badges and tent pegging equipment about. The show jumpers had bedded the yearling down in the mounted police lines. Worse, they had bedded him down in their kitchen. The stable hadn't been empty at all. Along one wooden wall were ranged provision stores and a full-sized calor-gas cooker. When I arrived, the yearling was looking on in an interested way as a man in dark blue trousers and a string vest was cooking his breakfast.

It could all have been extremely difficult; to my surprise it wasn't at all. The policeman grinned at me and shovelled his eggs and bacon onto a tin plate. He turned off the gas. "There you are, you see," he said to the yearling. "I told you yours would be along in a minute," and off he went.

Thinking Ahead

Thinking ahead involved the purchase of a hideously expensive, yearling filly of the right looks, movement and breeding, strapping it, mucking it out, feeding it and wringing our hands over it for three years, only to discover that in the meantime small daughter had grown into a stocky giantess whose size six boots (at eleven years old) hung level with its fine, elegant, little knees.

This discovery, coupled with the fact that not-so-small daughter had rather lost interest in show ponies and preferred to loaf around the fields on a fat, mud-caked little cob (which, admittedly, was more suited to her build anyway), necessitated an urgent rethink.

. . . her boots hung level with its fine, elegant, little knees

The rethink resulted in a decision to sell the bay mare with the white star, the pony we had imagined would take our daughter into the spotlight at the Horse of the Year Show and would now clearly not even take her to the end of the lane without its fine, elegant, little knees buckling under it from the strain.

We began to compose an advertisement. Word it as we might it sounded very flowery, very over done. It was only whilst we were composing the advertisement that we realised that all the things we were saying about our pony were actually true. Even in the cold light of day, without the benefit of rose-tinted spectacles, we really had a top class pony. We had another rethink. We decided to keep it.

Keeping it was one thing, showing it was quite another. We had our top class pony but we certainly didn't have a rider; not-so-small daughter was out of the question. In years gone by we had also had our fill of borrowed jockeys who, coached and cajoled in the art of ringcraft, had immediately left to ride a better pony, or gone off on a month's holiday leaving us with an empty saddle for our most important shows. No, there would be no borrowed jockey for our top class pony, we would have it professionally produced. The next problem was who would produce it.

About this time I was doing a series of interviews for a magazine which included a visit to a top class show pony yard. I liked it. I liked the immaculate stables, the contented-looking ponies, the loving, family atmosphere. I wanted to ask them if they would take my four-year-old but somehow the opportunity never arose. Time was running out. Finally, as they were running their prospects for the season up and down a beautiful lawn for my inspection, and their very best pony, champion everywhere and Pony of the Year came trotting past, I blurted out, "Oh, I've got one just like that at home!"

There was a bit of a silence after this. It is an in-joke in the showing world that everyone at the ringside has one just like the winner at home, except that it usually turns out to be cross-eyed or bandy-legged or worse.

The owners of the top class show pony yard were carefully polite about the one at home. They weren't at all keen to see it. They weren't even prepared to come and look. Out of good manners though, they agreed to cast an eye over it if I brought it to a show where they were exhibiting. All of which was somewhat damaging to our self-confidence.

In the days that followed I lost my appetite and at nights I lay sleepless in my bed. My husband pretended not to care, going around saying things like, "Well, if they don't recognise a champion when they see one, that's their loss, not ours." But secretly we both wondered if we had oversold our mare; if, after all this, she was just a rather plain, bay, pony. Suddenly, alarmingly, she looked just that.

On the day before the show I spent hours polishing and strapping the four-year-old, who was surprised to find herself the object of such attention. I washed her tail, tidied her mane and scrubbed and oiled her hooves. I dressed her in our most becoming day rug with matching bandages and buckled on a brass-mounted headcollar buffed to a high gloss with boot polish. My husband refused to come with me. I loaded the pony into the trailer and drove off, sick with fright.

During the journey, my doubts about the mare multiplied threefold. Rattling through Slough with all the lights on red, I became certain that the top people would groan and close their eyes and reel back, thinking that she was just too awful for words. My little mare became, on that drive, a monster, a freak of nature; and I almost turned back twice.

When I arrived at the show and lowered the ramp and saw her looking at me expectantly with her ears pricked and her perfect star shining, I was ashamed of myself for doubting her. The top people never doubted her for an instant. They took one look at her and loaded her into their five-star horse box. I drove home with my empty trailer not knowing whether to laugh or cry.

Two years later I sat on a plush seat and watched her canter round in the spotlight at the Horse of the Year Show as the crowd in the indoor arena did a slow handclap. The band played, the polished hooves flew, and rosettes fluttered from both sides of her bridle. My name was in the programme as joint owner, but someone else was waiting for her in the little collecting ring and someone else's child was in the saddle. It was not quite as I had planned it when thinking ahead.

Now, The Reflections of a Show(wo)man

It is only in retrospect that one comes to realise how transient, elusive and futile are the joys of the show ring. Safely distanced from the emotion of the moment, how easy it is to see that one suffered far, far too much when the rewards were so painfully few; when at the end of the day, spent up, burned up, and perhaps a little grown up, all one has to show for a substantial slice of one's life is a row of trophies along the dresser to which, with duster and long term silver polish, one will be a slave until the end of one's days.

I have seen enough of shows to last me a lifetime. If I never see another it will be all to the good. And if, by chance, I ever find myself becoming nostalgic about my showing days, I shall have a store of memories filed away against that moment, the re-running of which will banish all trace of misty-eyed sentiment and bring about a smart return to common sense.

The show ring in summer may have its fleeting pleasures but the wintering of show ponies certainly has none. Oh, how I hated the

. . . wild-eyed, ungrateful brutes

winters. I loathed trailing about in the mud and the snow, blue-nosed and quaking with aching, numbing cold, labouring with bales of hay and buckets of feed for wild-eyed, ungrateful brutes who galloped up, spraying me with dirt, shoving and pushing me about, squealing and kicking at each other, and giving me crafty nips when I was not looking in case, for one misguided moment, I had imagined that they actually liked me. One could be forgiven for wondering if the fat, shaggy and filthy beasts scrapping over their feeds in the mud were really the same creatures who, sleek and refined, gazed winningly from last year's proof copies of show snaps sent in by dozens of keen but disappointed photographers. Perhaps some of the time they were not, having been exchanged for others of a more common variety when one's attentions were elsewhere. Certainly during the winters, I would have been too cold and too miserable to care.

The field shelter springs to mind. It had seemed essential to the comfort and well-being of show ponies, roughed off and turned out for the winter. My husband was doubtful. The bank balance was not encouraging. Nevertheless catalogues were sent for, a large open fronted shelter was ordered, the site was prepared. The appearance of the shelter at the start of the winter was greeted by its potential inhabitants with expressions of horror and mistrust. Its contents, the deep litter bedding, the hay rack, the salt block, warranted only a disdainful sniff and a wholesale retreat to the far end of the field where the whole affair could be regarded with disapproval. Nights were spent, as before, in the shelter afforded by the trees that overhung part of the post and rail fencing. Frosts, gales, rain or snow could not tempt them.

I have sold my bicycle. It was not worth a great deal at the end of the day. It had suffered badly from the occasion when I was leading an excitable little pony from it and met the Meynell Hunt battering along the lane en route to the first draw of the day.

Passing motorists were fascinated by the sight of small ponies being led out on road work in their stable garments. "Poorly is it?" they would say, nodding sympathetically at the bandages and crawling alongside, edging me towards the nettle-filled ditch and holding up all subsequent traffic. Motorists in general have never heard of show ponies; therefore by their reckoning any equine special enough to be walked out in a rug, providing its legs are not long enough to make it a race-horse, must be a show jumper. How tired I became of trying to explain exactly what a show pony was and that no, they didn't really have to jump fences, or win races, or pull a carriage, and it was really nothing to do with eventing at all; and no, we very rarely competed against Harvey Smith or Princess Anne. They tended to lose interest after that.

I shall have no fond memories of the annual clothing inspection. The resignation of holding up last season's hideously expensive showing garments against next season's not-so-small daughter, knowing full well that no matter how cunningly I lengthened and widened, they still wouldn't fit.

There will not be too many shows that I will care to remember but I shall not easily forget what my husband said to me after getting out of bed at two in the morning in order to drive to the Royal Welsh Agricultural Show at Builth Wells for our class at nine o'clock, only to discover on our arrival that I had misread the schedule and it was not until noon. Nor shall I easily live down the time we turned up at Bakewell on the wrong day, and when we arrived at Shropshire and West, prepared the pony for the class, and discovered that we had forgotten to bring the saddle.

There was our totally forgettable performance at Windsor. "I can't see any small ponies about," I commented to a friend who was idly watching me get the pony ready. "I expect it will be a small class." She shrieked with laughter at such a show of ignorance. "Haven't you seen the catalogue?" she cried. "There are sixty-seven ponies entered!"

"Very funny," I said dryly, never receptive to humour just before the start of a class.

Sixty-seven ponies in the preliminary judging ring at Windsor is not very funny at all. Our pony, whose greatest successes have been achieved by good manners, became upset when she was forced to walk with an angrily swishing tail in her face and the pony behind resting its nose on her rump. She began to shuffle sideways and in doing so trod on my foot. I yelped with pain and accidentally caught her under the girth with my cane. She jumped in the air with an enraged squeal like a stuck pig, being in season at the time and feeling rather highly-strung. Small daughter, never one to be calm in an emergency, began to scream.

We were hemmed in with ponies, in front, behind and at both sides. The little mare didn't like it. She began to *piaffer*, lifting each tiny hoof as high as she could with clockwork precision. People at the ropes began to snigger. My foot hurt. I imagined my toe, crushed beyond recognition, quite possibly broken off altogether. I wanted to go home, but a piece of text from the BSPS rule book danced in front of my eyes. *A pony may not be led or ridden out of the ring without permission of the judge.*

My husband was no help. He stood at the ringside and when we bucketed past him, he covered his eyes with his hands. Eventually I tucked small daughter under my arm and limped up to the judges with the pony prancing at my side, her head up and her tail flying like a pennant. As I begged leave to retire there was a universal rustling at the ropes as hundreds of spectators looked us up in the catalogue, and sixty-six exhibitors watched our ignominious departure with eyes which clearly said, "Well, that's one less!"

Outside the ring the pony immediately reverted to her customary mild and obedient self, small daughter blew her nose, clambered back into the saddle and rode her unaided back to the horse box, but we drove home in a silence which lasted two days.

All of this happened many years ago, but the scars of this and other eventualities too painful to relate, still remain. There have been other ponies since, bigger ones and better ones, it must be said; but passions run highest in the show ring, and the humiliations are the greatest when one's children and one's ponies are tiny and vulnerable and one stands in the ring alongside them. There is, after all, no-one to blame for their failures and misfortunes but oneself. And wait, because this is not the end of it.

Not even my worst enemy could accuse me of being mercenary. Parsimony is not in my nature. But in the course of idle calculations, and adding up the cost of the purchase of, the feeding and transporting of, the equipping and entry fees of show ponies, even allowing for the deduction of sales of, and receipt of occasional prize money won by these same ponies, I have discovered that each rosette on my dresser has cost me an average of £250, and that includes the pink ones. The pearl of the collection, the Royal Windsor Championship, came rather more expensive, say £750.

So there you have it, if you value your peace of mind, your husband, your sanity and your friendly bank manager, do not become a showing parent. Keep well away from the show ring. But if you would like to have the end result, without all the hassle it entails, I have some slightly flyblown rosettes for sale, at a *fraction* of their actual value . . .

KNOWING ABOUT SHOWING

There is no real mystique about producing horses and ponies for the show ring. Showing people may have the reputation of being artful and secretive, but in my days as an exhibitor and a roving reporter I never found them so. If, in the paddock, one espied a pony cantering around festooned with draw and side-reins and its mouth full of string, or if every horse in the yard appeared to be wearing a fur-lined bonnet, there was always someone happy to explain why.

The truth is that it is not often that a horse or pony is so naturally perfect that it needs no artificial help whatsoever, but the same could be said of humans after all. A top showing yard is rather like a model school for equines; it's amazing what a bit of professional grooming and a few sharp lessons in deportment and good manners can achieve. In the equine model schools, where miracles are wrought daily, pig's ears are sent out to win looking remarkably like princesses. The end result is obtained by means of much grinding hard work and minute attention to detail. Only a handful of amateur producers have the know-how and the dedication to do the same, which is why, when a top animal changes hands, it will more often than not plummet to obscurity.

I always think that Wembley is a microcosm of the showing world. The part of the Horse of the Year Show that the public sees is very glamorous; the gleaming coats of the horses in the spotlights, the immaculate riders in their navy and their scarlet, the satin rosettes and the silver trophies. They have no idea that a few yards away people are hobbling around outside with gravel in their shoes; that in the preliminary judging these same elegant animals floundered round fetlock-deep in sand, or on circles of black ash from which the dust rose in clouds, obliterating carefully chalked socks on the first circuit; that during their run-up for conformation and action on the concrete, a coach was likely to disgorge thirty-five strolling persons between the exhibit and the judge; or that people with buckets and sticks wait outside to grab and dope-test the winners as soon as they hit daylight, whipping the samples off by Securicor down the North Circular to Newmarket. Showing people maintain that it's the sighs of relief after Wembley that blow the leaves off the trees!

The onlooker may see most of the game, but I wouldn't have missed for anything, my years inside the rails, and without them I certainly wouldn't have been able to write the three pieces which come next.

Where Have All the Show Folk Gone . . . ?

It is a commonly held fallacy that the showing fraternity, like foxes, go to earth in the winter. This is a misleading legend because showing people can be discovered all over the place providing you know where to look. For instance, throughout the festive season they are to be found outside any party, clutching large gins and counting the rosettes in the tack room, chortling over the draw-reins, the underchecks, overchecks and Abbott Davies balancing-reins in evidence, and surreptitiously checking the age of any show exhibit obliging enough to open its mouth.

The British Show Pony Society Ball is positively alive with showing people of the pony variety who may seem even more eccentric than any other kind. The leading-rein strain can be easily picked out in motion, having developed a peculiar gliding gait all of their own, and the first ridden species can be distinguished by the fact that their fingernails are all bitten to the quick. Owners of the larger ridden pony can be identified by the permanent chalk marks at 12.2, 13.2 and 14.2, just above the left lapel for instant measurement of the opposition.

On dark, dreary, winter days which are notoriously bad for spotting showing people, a few hardy specimens can sometimes be lured out by a carefully worded advertisement in *Horse & Hound* (*Absolutely* Top Class . . . to knowledgeable showing home *only*), and now and again you may be lucky enough to catch sight of one or two lurking in the hedgerows, disguised in old mackintoshes, hoping to glimpse a rival's new exhibit for the coming season.

Occasionally the odd one will appear in the hunting field, or by some unfortunate accident, on it. The showing person, being skilled in the art of dress and turn out, shines at the meet and will even be photographed graciously accepting a murky stirrup cup whilst keeping a sharp eye out for the gin. Rarely however, do they survive the first good run of the day, because other than in the working hunter class when there is a prize in the offing, the showing person is not usually noted for his performance across country, being far too worried about curbs, splints, windgalls and throughpins and other unsightly signs of wear and tear in his exhibit, ever to become a Hard Person to Hounds. The showing person also dislikes having his immaculate turn out splashed with mud or, even worse, blood. As one showing person commented to me recently as we rode off together in search of a convenient gate, "It isn't the height of the hedge that worries me, it's the forty-three others behind me, all heading for the same place."

After the festivities, in late January and February, showing people are mainly to be found at the larger ironmongers where they are to be seen purchasing vast quantities of heavy gauge polythene to fashion into neck and shoulder sweaters for over-weight equines, tubes of pollyfilla with which to plaster over the sandcracks, and quantities of small screws to enable them to transfer the infra-red heaters from the bathroom to the stables. With a pair of efficient binoculars (and perhaps in some cases, a conveniently placed ladder) showing people can also be sighted in their own kitchens, lovingly concocting nasty glue-like potions surrounded by egg shells and treacle. The finished product will be expected to tempt a potential showring exhibit who has had his equilibrium temporarily upset by being suddenly transferred from a frozen paddock to a stable bedded eyebrow-deep in straw with an infra-red heater turned on full pelt.

About the first of March, any reputable riding clothiers will be humming with showing people of every variety who will demand impossibly tight breeches and jodhpurs in this year's most fashionable colour, which, if the proprietor is well stocked with lemon, will be cream or white or vice versa. They will break, on average, three zippers for every pair of jodhpurs purchased, and will demand navy blue or black riding gloves which do not, and never have existed. Riding pony people, who consider themselves as trendsetters in the show ring, will order bespoke showing jackets for their riders in puce and dove grey with contrasting velvet collars, and then blame the shop when they are unable to find headgear to match. Hack people, who like to imagine themselves as slender and elegant, will order high boots thinner and longer than their own legs in order to preserve the illusion of having "a good leg for a boot" and will complain bitterly because they are impossible to put on. The very last straw will be the leading-rein people who appear with frighteningly tiny children who bite the assistants, swallow the thimble, refuse to be measured, howl the place down and worse. The wise riding clothier will take his annual holidays in March, and since all orders for showing people must be completed within a week or sooner, he will be very little bothered with them the rest of the year.

Saddlers and their apprentices will all be working overtime at this time of year fashioning short-seated saddles with cut-back flaps for compact cobs with no shoulders, constructing saddles with extended seats and shortened flaps for hunters with long backs and no depth to speak of, and stitching acres of pimpled rubber to the underside of lampwick girths to prevent surgical saddles from creeping inexorably forwards. Bridles made from bootlaces will be turned out by the thousand for riding pony people to whom all experienced saddlers pretend to be totally deaf and mute to forestall any argument, knowing full well that whatever they produce cannot possibly be thin enough or dark enough or ready soon enough to satisfy them.

A month before the first show, the blacksmith's forge will be crowded with showing people who have booked in their exhibits for pathological shoeing. They will demand shoes which are built-up, built-down, and built-up-and-down. Some will want shoes heavier, shoes lighter, and shoes that are heavy and light at the same time. Others who are well-versed in the art of deception to a fine degree will have already marked the spot on their exhibits' hooves where the clips are to be placed with chalk, thus, by an optical illusion, making their pin-toed or splay-footed equine appear to stand four square.

Two weeks, or sometimes two days before the show comes the showing person's annual transport inspection, after which showing people may be observed at their local garages, stamping their feet and shouting rather a lot due to flat batteries, binding brakes, rat-gnawed tyres, rusted springs and corroded terminals, none of which can possibly be their fault because the horse box hasn't been used for at least six months.

Leading-rein people who often attach their trailer to the company car may not be too much bothered by engine trouble, being merely undecided as to whether to paint the trailer to match the Cortina or stain it mahogany to match the pony.

Naturally, after the first show of the season, showing people become positively commonplace and of interest only to judges, fellow exhibitors and bank managers; the latter being rather likely to worry dreadfully over the escalating overdrafts of showing people during the season due to the cost of petrol and entry fees as opposed to the pathetic return in prize money, which, in any case, is usually spent in the beer tent after the class. The beer tent is one of the chief habitats of showing people during the summer and outside the showground, they are often to be sighted parked outside *Little Chefs* and being towed off the M1, the A1 and similar stretches of motorway due to their vehicles having blown tyres, blown gaskets or blown up altogether.

From all this it may be deduced that being a showing person is no joke. They are not, however, a threatened species; in fact recent statistics show that they are on the increase, which must be good news for somebody.

Showing a Sense of Humour

"Showing," a friend once said to me, as we stood together at the bottom of the line at one of the larger agricultural shows, "is not so much What You Show, as Who You Know," and with this perceptive statement (delivered in a very loud voice) he grasped his two-year-old filly by the bridle and stalked out of the ring under the disapproving gaze of a top judge, a long line of fellow exhibitors and half-a-million or so spectators.

As one who has often been found scuffling about disconsolately at the wrong end of the line, practising false smiles with which to receive the dreaded pink rosette, I can sympathise with his point of view, but I have never been courageous enough (or rude enough) to do the same.

Of course, every in-hand showing person knows that the secret of truly successful judging is to ignore the exhibit entirely and to concentrate upon the attendant. If the attendant is a well known showing person, this will immediately move the pony up three places even if it moves like a flail. The fact that the attendant is nattily turned out in good tweed and cavalry twill (in-hand classes) or a navy suit with a bowler hat (leading-rein) will bring it up another two even if its head resembles a turnip. Any display of olde worlde courtesy by the attendant directed at the judge, such as raising the hat, picking up her glove or mentioning that they just happen to be a fifteenth cousin, twice removed, of the Queen Mother, will immediately secure a rosette, possibly a red, white and blue one.

Quite the easiest way to judge an attendant though, is on the move. The attendant should cover the ground lightly and easily, in a fluid, graceful movement, not showing too much knee and keeping level with the equine's shoulder with the chin well up whilst holding the end of the leading-rein as if proffering a plate of cucumber sandwiches. As one might expect from this description, the effect is often more easily achieved by a female attendant, although certain types of gentlemen can do it extremely well. An overtly camp performance is not really recommended however, as some judges consider it to be in slightly suspect taste. A really fine run up by the attendant can bring an exhibit into the first three, even if it can accommodate three people between withers and rump.

Standing in line whilst a class of horrific proportions perform their individual run-ups though, can be a tedious business, especially if you are not near the top – where the view is distinctly better, especially if it includes a silver cup. However, the monotony can be relieved by a close examination of one's fellow exhibitors, who will not be aware of the fact, being far too engrossed in examining other fellow exhibitors to notice.

. . . certain gentlemen in the hack classes

Beginner riders in the show ring can be picked out at once as having perfectly delightful buttonholes consisting of a full blown rose accompanied by dense foliage and maidenhair fern, all nicely done up in Bacofoil, all of which would do justice to a provincial wedding but in the show ring is not quite the thing. Certain gentlemen in the hack classes affect a carnation and a voluminous, highly-coloured, spotted handkerchief with which to mop their brows in a theatrical manner whilst being careful not to disturb their

. . . the hunting farmer

makeup. The hunting farmer is easy to pick out in the hunter classes, having a check tweed jacket worn with a buff waistcoat and brown boots together with a bowler hat and a false red nose to add a touch of authenticity to the proceedings. For practicality though, the in-hands take some beating, for during one very wet season, one exhibitor, becoming fed up with wet socks, carefully died his ankles black, and one well-known leading-rein competitor has been growing cress round the brim of his bowler hat for two seasons.

Conversing in line to pass the time is frowned upon by many experienced exhibitors who will refuse to talk back, thus making any conversation rather one-sided. Humming, whistling or singing is not encouraged either, although chinking coins and musical match boxes are a well-known aid in the ridden pony classes.

Many small ponies fall asleep whilst waiting in line, as do small children, and their attendants can be seen poking them awake with a leather-covered cane carried for the purpose. Hack exhibitors are allowed to read their correspondence and newspapers whilst waiting in line as a legacy from the days when proper gentlemen perused their mail whilst riding their hacks through Hyde Park. One famous exhibitor opened his electricity bill by mistake and was subsequently felled by a heart attack in the middle of his figure eight. Leading-rein children, unable to endure the long wait, pretend a desire to visit the loo and sometimes creep away undetected. Many an attendant has performed an impeccable run-up in front of the judge, only to be bitterly disappointed to discover that the rider was not actually in the saddle, but waiting contentedly back in line with his tie round the back of his neck and covered with chocolate ice-cream purchased by a rival exhibitor.

A small flask of gin used to provide artificial cheer at the bottom end of the line during interminable judging sessions, as many an exhibitor discovered in the past, when any presence lacked by the exhibit was more than compensated for by the rider who performed many startling feats during his individual show. This improved the viewing appeal of the showing classes substantially and people were actually weaned away from the show-jumping rings. But the showing societies took the view that such goings-on vulgarised the classes and reduced them to the level of a circus. They showed their disapproval by bringing in a new rule which forbade the use of any artificial stimulants whatsoever and introduced breathalyser and dope tests in the collecting rings, which was a source of bitter disappointment to many exhibitors.

Currently there is a vogue for 'bored' games at the bottom of the line and riders carry miniature draughts and chessmen in their pockets which is why so many show horses and ponies have checkerboard rumps. Backgammon is also a popular pastime, played on the sharks-teeth markings applied to the flanks.

Idiosyncratic and long-winded though the showing classes may be, they are an essential part of our horse shows, none of which would be complete without them. And as for show exhibitors, well, they are all jolly good folk; charming, unselfish and totally sportsmanlike. Any show exhibitor will tell you the same.

Dear Disgruntled . . .

Dear Disgruntled,

I'm sorry to have to start off a new season by getting the stick out, but I *do* wish you wouldn't keep writing to *Horse & Hound* signing yourself Disgruntled Showing Exhibitor. The showing fraternity already have the reputation of being a collection of yellow-eyed grumblers but, quite frankly, your last letter takes the biscuit.

I mean, it won't do you any good at all to keep carping on about escalating entry fees. What can we do about it? Yes, I agree that an entry fee of ten pounds and a first prize of four pounds and fifty pence isn't too inviting, but you do get a single-tier rosette as well, and inflation is hitting the show classes as well as everything else. We all have to tighten our girths. We all have to suffer. Sometimes I wonder who you think you are anyway. You don't exactly pull the crowds you know; two ten-year olds and a golden labrador don't add up to a main ring attraction in anybody's book.

Then there's the little matter of the joint measurement scheme. I suppose that's our fault as well. I do realise that it's jolly hard luck to be measured out of the class by one eighth of an inch just because somebody sneezed at the wrong moment, but I would hardly term it victimisation. Well, I know the horse cost you thousands and now it's out of the class and your career is in ruins, but why not try again? The JMS will be delighted to give you another chance. After all, they only want to be fair. I'm sure they will be delighted to bring the mobile measurement unit out especially; all they need is a nice level surface and no distractions to get the horse up on its toes – how about Battersea Fun Fair, or the entrance to the Dartford Tunnel on a Friday night?

I suppose your show specimens have wintered out this year? I wonder if people know that to the showing fraternity 'wintering out' means from touchdown after Wembley until Boxing Day? I wonder if they also know that you wrap your equines in polythene corsets to slim them down, or force-feed them like pâté-geese to fatten them up? No, of course I'm not prejudiced against showing people, whatever made you think that?

. . . the final judging will be outside this year

You realise, of course, that there won't be any cups to win this year? Those that haven't been stolen are needed for the show-jumping. Even at Wembley I'm afraid you will have to be content with a replica of a replica.

And speaking of Wembley, you have heard that the final judging is to be outside this year? It does seem a little hard, I know, but there simply isn't enough room inside for everyone, and hacks, hunters and ponies are just *not* good TV material. Yes, I do realise it will be dark, but there are excellent lights in the multi-storey car park and they do reflect; and every judge will be provided with a really powerful torch.

Well, if you're going to be like that about it . . . No wonder showing people have such a poor image!

Some people are never satisfied. Don't think I don't know that you were one of the leaders of the campaign to bring in dope testing for the show classes. Now you have the nerve to complain about it. Yes, I can quite see that it might have been an embarrassment to be tested on three consecutive occasions whilst all the other exhibitors stood round and sniggered, but it was purely coincidental. And no, there doesn't seem to be a more refined way of going about it other than a bucket on a stick, so you will just have to put up with it. And as for lodging an objection because when you insisted on being present at the next draw, they drew the names of both of your exhibits out of the hat, it's clearly ridiculous. *Of course* all the other names went in, it was just the luck of the draw. All I can say about it is you wanted dope testing, you've got it.

Whilst I'm about it, I've some more news for you. You know the major show where the committee rules that if you win a prize on the first day, you have to stay and compete in the Championship of Championships on the second or forfeit your prize money? And you remember that they let you house your exhibit free of charge in the little wooden stable with the bit of sacking for a top door? Well, this year you've got to pay. Now, don't be silly. After all, if you're prepared to travel a hundred and seventy miles in that luxury mobile horse hotel with hot and cold showers and interior sprung mattresses, doing a bare twelve miles to the gallon, and pay ten pounds to enter the class, what's another thirteen pounds fifty on top of that? And it's only if you *win*, if you don't, you won't need to stay anyway; you'll actually save money.

Now there's no need to be abusive. I'd watch my step if I were you. Two can play at that game. Don't imagine for a minute that your secrets are safe from us. We know all about the pathological shoeing and the pollyfilla in the sandcracks. Not to mention the surgical saddles, the toe weights and the jowl sweaters. One more letter to the editor signed 'Disgruntled Showing Exhibitor' and we might just spill the beans.

Then you *will* have something to complain about . . .

(Not) The Editor,
Horse & Hound.

ORGANISING SECRETARY

More fraught than any other aspect of showing is the organisation of a show. In my riding school days we had a show every month from April to October. It nearly always rained. One of my clearest memories is of standing outside the ungainly, Victorian house in Burton-on-Trent (there's a housing estate in its place now), staring up at the sky saying, "It's definitely brighter," in heartening tones, whilst the rain poured ceaselessly out of the leaden sky. Rain or not, I was always desperately anxious that everyone should have a good time and there were plenty of prizes. My mother maintained that mine were the only shows where you could win a cup for failing to enter the ring in the jumping.

Organising a small show is however, a piece of cake compared to organising a mammoth one. I was once appointed secretary to a large one-day show in the Midlands. Oh, I have some tales to tell about my days as a show secretary! About the farmer who entered a pig and let down the ramp of his suspiciously large cattle wagon to reveal twenty-three of his friends and relations seated on beer crates. About the motor cycle display team who only just failed to clear six parked cars (the sixth belonged to the show chairman). About the day the grandstand collapsed with everybody in it. About the day the parachutists dropped through low cloud and drifted gently down into the cattle lines and the lake, whilst the crowd around the main ring gazed fruitlessly heavenwards. Then there was the memorable occasion when the interminable stream of cars through the main entrance astonished the British Legion gatemen by refusing to pay. Hadn't they already paid once, the drivers cried indignantly, displaying raffle tickets to prove it, sold to them by a con-man with a canvas bag up on the main road.

There was the day the portacabin loos ran out of flatpacks before ten in the morning because somebody had walked off with the two hundred I had provided the night before. Some members of the committee maintained that I had forgotten to order them.

But this was nothing in comparison to the panic every year over returned trophies. Exhibitors regularly *mislaid* solid silver cups or sent them back through the ordinary mail with a luggage label attached to one of the handles. I once received a black plinth with four golden hooves upon it; the rest of the horse was missing, neatly snapped off at the fetlocks. The post office denied all responsibility. The show committee voted it all my fault.

The pieces that follow tell similar stories based not only on the organisation of shows, but of other doomed events, inspired by a short period on the committee of a Hunt Supporters' Club.

A Show Secretary Speaks

I have threatened to resign a million times, but body and soul can stand only so much and I have finally given up the secretaryship of the agricultural show. In retrospect, I emerge filled with admiration for the many secretaries, show councils and committees who organise similar events all over the country, often at great inconvenience to themselves and for no financial reward.

That there were rewards to be had could be in no doubt, if only because the show committee constantly told me so. "Of course," they would say, "it isn't well paid as a *job*, but it's very *rewarding* work." When asked to be more specific about the kind of rewards I could expect, however, they became vague and evasive. With hindsight I suspect they meant that I would be rewarded in Heaven, but I hadn't envisaged having to wait that long.

The aforementioned hindsight is one of the most important qualifications for a show secretary, as is foresight and second sight.

Eyesight is not so important and can be a positive disadvantage as all kinds of errors can be excused by poor eyesight, but the lack of fore, hind and second sight will not be forgiven. For example, a show secretary is expected to sense immediately that a tradesman who describes his merchandise on the stand space application form as 'fine quality sheepskin goods', is actually peddling nasty, black spiders on sticks which will lower the tone of the show and bring complaints from neighbouring standholders that the whole show is in danger of being reduced to a fun-fair.

A small knowledge of arithmetic is desirable in a show secretary, although those who are worried about working out complicated lactation figures for the cattle yield classes will be relieved to hear that farmers are delighted to work out their own figures, especially if they have seen everyone else's first.

Craft is essential in a show secretary as there is no-one in the world so crafty as a trader or an exhibitor, or even a spectator. The only possible way to stay on top of the job is to become even more cunning and crafty than they are. Tact is also vitally important as this can save time, money, and occasionally, lives. Many feel that it is not tactful to exhibit at your own show, especially if you chose the judge yourself; however, taking into consideration the fact that any winning entry not immediately recognised by the rest of the exhibitors will be explained away as belonging to the secretary, one may as well enter anyway.

Organising ability is a virtue shared by all great secretaries but one need not be able to make important decisions as generally, the larger the show, the fewer decisions are made by the secretary. All major policy is decided by a council, split into various committees. It is only in any kind of emergency that the secretary is left holding the can.

As any show secretary knows, horse and pony classes cause their own special problems. While entries in other sections diminish, these classes continue to swell to horrific proportions. The classes themselves are dealt with on show day by an army of specially trained stewards who have preferably completed a commando course. This will enable them to pacify screaming children and the occasional parent, tie hair-ribbons and catch loose ponies in the leading-rein class; dodge flailing hooves and teeth in the in-hand classes; evict dogs from the arena, and prevent small boys from fishing in the water jump.

Entry forms need close attention for these classes as horse and pony exhibitors make all sorts of mistakes when filling them in. Careful study of the catalogues of other shows will reveal many errors, including animals whose height, age and sire change from week to week. Horse and pony exhibitors are suspicious of the fact that age must be determined by date of birth, preferring to fix their own to suit the class and making their exhibits' birthdays a movable feast to enable them to enter both yearling and two-year-old classes having, amazingly, jotted down their exact hour of birth which fell conveniently between the two classes.

Beginners in the show ring often make the most spectacular mistakes and may genuinely believe their twenty-five year old gelding is eligible for a brood mare premium, and may be quite reluctant to remove the family donkey from the leading-rein class when asked to leave the ring by the steward. A novice class will cause many an exhibitor to have a complete mental blockage and people who have been exhibiting for years will innocently enter animals who have won all over the country.

Luckily, the secretary can safely leave this sort of situation to the eagle-eyes of fellow exhibitors who, far from closing in to protect their own, will come leaping in droves to the tent, waving their catalogues and uttering shrill cries of outrage. Some may even rush off home to unearth yellowing copies of *Horse & Hound* with which to substantiate their complaint.

Trade stands are a cause of much anguish for the secretary. The major exhibitors are slowly withdrawing their support from large agricultural shows owing to the high cost of assuaging the thirst of farmers who, though professing a lively interest, would no more buy a combine harvester than fly to the moon. That the few remaining exhibitors are feeling the pinch is obvious to any show secretary on show day when their representatives may be found in the early hours of the morning applying cheap scotch to the turf around their stands to act as bait.

Good public relations are perhaps the most important asset to the show secretary. Public relations are nothing to do with one's own family, as all the best secretaries have no family and no friends at all, thus remaining entirely impartial. The image of the dedicated secretary should be modest and even rather shabby. The show committee will be suspicious of the smallest display of personal expenditure or extravagance. The purchase of a new car will result in the show accountant being summoned to inspect the books.

Relations with the press should be handled with great care as they are potential dynamite. Local newspaper reporters either encourage the public to come to the show, or see to it that they prefer to stay away. Some weeks prior to the show, the secretary should prepare a press release giving details of all the attractions the show has to offer. The report which will appear in print will be somewhat rearranged and will contain some charming errors. Competitors in the driving marathon will immediately scratch when they read that the length of the drive will be two hundred miles, and people will come from miles around to see the display of monsters put on by the Young Farmers, only to discover that the newspaper omitted the word onion from the report. Though the wise secretary will have kept a copy of the original press release, the show committee will never be entirely convinced that it wasn't made afterwards.

Any secretary seeking to reduce entries in the horse and pony classes should seriously consider helicopters as a main ring attraction. These are enormously popular with the general public who consider the landing quite spectacular when several hundredweight of dust, turf and even jumps may rise in the air. The formation teams can be just as thrilling, rivalled only by the antics of any livestock unfortunate enough to be around at the time.

Motor-cycle teams are eternally popular, especially with the young, mainly because of the noise they produce. The more proficient of the teams perform hair-raising tricks, such as driving through hoops of fire and leaping over thirty-six prone people, usually managing to clear at least thirty-four of them.

Free-fall parachuting is a magical event which can be upset by low cloud when the aeroplanes are unable to drop from the specified height and the parachutists may even land before the 'chute has had time to open. If the cloud is thin, they may decide to drop from above it thus occasioning some inaccuracy, when the public will be surprised to see parachutists descending amongst the pig pens or on top of the grandstand.

Hot air balloons can be eye-catching and dramatic but, unfortunately, they tend to be erratic as their progress is governed by atmospheric pressures and the prevailing winds. Some shows, having organised such attractions, have waited all day, staring up at the sky, only to see the balloonists carried past at high speeds owing to the unforecasted wind. Once it was reported that one unlucky member of the public received a nasty blow from an ill-timed sack of ballast which rendered him unconscious for three days.

Police displays with dogs, horses and road safety are popular entertainment, especially if one of the team is accidently bitten, falls off, or is run over. Fire-fighting can be spectacular in its way, but it is advisable to have this display as the finale to avoid masses of irate exhibitors paddling round in the grand parade.

Marching displays are colourful and can even be quite musical but they do need a large arena as the effect is rather lost if the width of the ring is only twelve marching strides across. Steer riding and rodeos can be dangerous for all concerned which is probably why the public like them so much. Insurance companies dislike steer riding as do the steers themselves.

Wild west rodeos are all very well, especially if you can persuade the show directors to have a go. But as everyone knows, most 'Wild West Broncos' are straight out of the New Forest and are not really wild at all; in fact, later on they may appear in the junior jumping.

Veteran cars, tractors and steam engines are a delight to the enthusiast but less so to others, mainly because of the voluminous clouds of smoke and the snails-pace progress; however the latter iron out the ground very well which must be regarded as a bonus. The prosperous show may be able to stage a trotting race as a main ring attraction, or even hire a show-jumping star to compete in the open jumping, but soon this will be out of the reach of all but a few.

Show committees like their secretaries to organise a prize draw in order to swell the funds and the wise secretary will avoid this like the plague, but will be lucky to escape at least one attempt. The first thing to do is to obtain a licence under the Small Lotteries Act from the local council. They will immediately suspect you of running it for your own personal benefit and will issue you with a flood of application forms, return forms, regulations and instructions, hoping to discourage you from taking the matter any farther.

You will next take delivery of what appears to be a terrifyingly large amount of tickets from the printer, who will personally present you with a hefty bill and insist on immediate payment, having been

. . . main ring attractions should be spectacular and dramatic

caught out by prize-draw organisers before. Thus, provided that you have been able to wring sufficient prizes out of the committee, all that remains is to sell the tickets which, if it happens to be Christmas, Easter, Hallowe'en, Bonfire Night or any time in between, will be almost impossible.

Everyone you approach with a book of tickets will smile knowingly and, crying, "Snap!" produce a book of his own tickets which he will be prepared to swop for a book of yours. This can lead to all sorts of distressing complications and when filling in the return form for the local council, the legend under 'profits', which reads fourteen pounds and seventy pence, two tea cloths, half a hundredweight of potatoes, a live turkey and two thousand unsuccessful prize-draw tickets (various charities) at five pence each, will be sufficient to send the chief clerk into a coma for days – which will just about serve him right.

An essential motto for a show secretary is *nil desperandum*, particularly when faced with the morning after a show held in the inevitable cloudburst when the expected gate of 21,000 becomes a miserable 250 and the local newspaper carries a front page photograph of a few, grey-faced people standing in a pool of water under the heading *Is This the End for the Show?*

The efficient secretary will be up on the show ground at an early hour. The ground will be a morass of mud and duckboards, tractor ruts, battered marquees and a sea of sodden paper cups and catalogues as far as the eye can see.

The press, who will appear in the hope of a good disaster story, or maybe even a suicide, should receive a strong drink immediately on arrival. This should be followed by as many as they can reasonably take and still be able to write their copy. Thus, if all goes according to plan, the headlines in the evening paper should read something like *Show undaunted by the worst weather for 75 years — Next year's show will be bigger and better than ever, says secretary.*

The inevitable aftermath of a show held in such diabolical weather conditions is that the landlord will not only demand payment for reseeding the ground and recompense for lost grazing, but will also give the show notice to quit the site. This is a very good time for the secretary to resign, as the problems of finding another site with suitable access, sufficient acreage and at a rent that the show council feel they can afford are insurmountable!

A Substitute Judge

"If Mrs Clarke-Jones is on the showground, will she please hasten to ring three, where her class is waiting?"

The announcement was relayed to the outer car park, where the Royal British Legion waved motorists into precise positions marked with a plumb line. It reached the pig lines on the opposite side of the park, where white-coated judges clustered round an in-pig gilt and chewed their ball point pens. It was audible in the horse box park, where children and ponies were being schooled by over-anxious parents. The roundabouts and sideshows were still sheeted, but the solitary man in Happyland heard it as he stocked his booth with furry monkeys fashioned from the pelts of dead rabbits.

The WI, laying out iced cakes and needlework heard it, as did the beekeepers, the horticultural society, and the officials of the exemption dog show. It was heard by many people doing many things, but not by Mrs Clarke-Jones, which was hardly surprising because she had lost her fan-belt on the A1.

The chief steward advanced towards my table for the fifth time in as many minutes. Stewards for pony classes are hand picked for *sang froid* but his voice was not without a trace of agitation. He said, "You'll have to do something, miss. The natives is getting restless."

The secretary's tent faced the collecting ring. I could see only too well the drooping heads of ponies who had already lost their sparkle, the children who had waited too long, their expectancy turned to fretfulness and the watching faces of the parents, impatient and angry.

"Most certainly something will have to be done." I did my best to sound decisive. I scanned the immediate vicinity for the show director but with scant hope of success; he was in the further regions of the showground, called in to arbitrate between two farmers, each accusing the other of fiddling figures in the dairy yield classes.

"We shall have to find a substitute judge," I decided.

The chief steward brightened, but only for a moment. "Where from?" he enquired, backing off in alarm. "Oh *no*, not me, miss! Not leading-rein! Oh no, miss, you *wouldn't*!"

In the midst of these protestations fate, in the guise of Henry Hornchurch, stepped in. The ingratiating little man decked out in breeches, brown boots and a check jacket was a stranger to me. I fancied the chief steward was not so ill-aquainted. He grew rather agitated and stood behind the newcomer frowning most severely and shaking his head.

"Good morning to you, miss," Henry Hornchurch leaned forward to give me the full benefit of a not entirely toothless smile. "I hear you're in a spot of bother, so to speak."

I moved my chair a little further back. "We do appear to be without a judge for the small pony classes," I admitted.

"Then this is your lucky day," Henry Hornchurch patted my hand in a familiar manner. "Here am I, Henry Hornchurch, a lifetime's experience of horses behind me, you-name-it-and-I've-judged-it, on the spot and at your service."

Such camaraderie from a complete stranger was unnerving. In addition, the chief steward continued his performance, alternately covering his eyes with his hands, stabbing his finger at Henry Hornchurch and shaking his head vigorously.

In other circumstances I might have heeded him, but out of the corner of my eye I saw a bowler-hatted figure approaching the tent. The figure had a face like an angry, red balloon and it was dragging behind it a small grey pony on which sat a squalling infant.

"Please ask the class to enter the ring," I said firmly to the chief steward. "Inform them that a substitute judge has been appointed."

The chief steward shrugged his shoulders in a 'Well, don't say I didn't try to warn you' manner, and marched off, somewhat tight-lipped, to turn back the envoy. I collected up the award box and the judge's book and prepared to take over the forward marking of the catalogue.

. . . stabbing his finger and shaking his head vigorously

As Henry Hornchurch took up his position in the ring, the effect on exhibitors was electric. Several steered their charges towards him, ascertained that it was truly he, and walked out. It was an unpromising start, but the substitute judge was not upset. "That makes the job a bit easier, anyhow," he said cheerfully. He put his hands on his hips and, brown boots straddled, surveyed what remained of the class in a leisurely manner.

"I hope the judging will not be prolonged, Mr Hornchurch," I said, "we must try to adhere to the programme, and already we are fifteen minutes behind schedule."

"Your word is my command," Henry Hornchurch said warmly, "I'll have them sorted out in no time at all." So saying, he moved forward and bellowed at the startled exhibitors. "Let's see a bit of action, now! Trot! Everybody trot! All together – trot on!"

It was obvious that you-name-it-and-I've-judged-it had not been the entire truth; plainly Henry Hornchurch had never before judged a leading-rein class.

"They don't usually trot together," I told him, "they trot individually." But my protest was lost in his enthusiastic chivvying of those who hesitated. "Come along there, trot on! We haven't got all day you know."

Unaccustomed to communal speed, the ponies either hung back reluctantly or set off with gusto, towing their attendants along the rails. The bowler-hatted envoy was carried past a roan pony who let fly with its heels. His tiny rider flew off and landed under the nose of the exhibit trotting along behind. The pony swerved to avoid treading on the child, cannoned into its own attendant and neatly pitched its jockey over its shoulder.

In the melee which followed, the chief steward plucked at my cardigan in an agony of anxiety. "Oh, miss," he groaned, "get him out of here."

"Now don't get upset," Henry Hornchurch was saying to the wailing children, "I'll pretend I didn't see that. Come along, now, let's have you back on top." He picked up the nearest child and placed it on the roan pony.

"Excuse me, but you've taken my jockey," the bowler-hatted man said. The substitute judge plucked the child off the roan and obligingly set it down on the grey.

"Nerves travel up the reins," he said helpfully to the little girl who was squeaking with fright.

By the time Henry Hornchurch had the class trotting to his satisfaction again, some of the attendants were looking decidedly worn.

"I really do feel they have trotted for long enough," I said.

"Yes, you could be right there," Henry Hornchurch said agreeably. He stepped forward. "Canter on now!" he shouted, "everybody canter!"

The chief steward looked as if he might pass out. I said weakly, "Mr Hornchurch, I feel I must point out that leading-rein ponies *never* canter."

The exhibitors had had enough. A lady in a plush hat dug in her heels so suddenly that her child was pitched forward onto the pony's neck. The rest of the class piled up behind, angry and bewildered.

"What the devil's happening?" someone wanted to know.

The chief steward found his voice. "Walk on, please," he commanded. "Walk on, the judge is about to make his selection."

With his hands on his hips, Henry Hornchurch surveyed the class before him. The well produced, quality ponies appeared to escape his notice entirely. He pointed to a sturdy grey with a roman nose which had lapped the other exhibits at a strong trot with a distinct trace of hackney. "I'll have that one first," he said. "It's a real good sort. You can see by the way the kid's boots only reach half-way down the saddle flaps that it will last her until she's at least twelve."

I was too surprised by this bicycle logic to make any comment. The grey's attendant dragged it into the centre of the ring, looking astonished and not a little suspicious, having never before been placed anywhere but in the back line.

"I'll have number forty-seven in next," Henry Hornchurch informed the chief steward, whose face was almost the colour of the award sheet in his hand. Number forty-seven was an ancient, little bay mare with loose hairy plaits, led on a red halter rope by an untidy dark-haired woman in a flowered blouse. As they passed the substitute judge on their way to take up the position next to the grey, I heard the child whisper, "Have I won a prize, Uncle Henry?" but Uncle Henry was busily selecting his third prize winner, a long-backed chestnut with a hogged mane and a glaringly new saddle and bridle. I could bear it no longer. Looking into the distance with a feigned anxiety, I hurried out of the ring as if I had noticed something which required my urgent and immediate attention.

In the secretary's tent I waited impatiently for the return of the show director who returned at last and smelled mightily of whisky. "Would it be all right if I went to lunch?" I asked him.

Over his broad shoulder I could see Henry Hornchurch holding out a placating hand to a small group of angry-looking people. A larger group were walking purposefully towards the tent. At their head was the man with the bowler hat.

"By all means you must go to lunch," the show director said benevolently. "I really had no idea what difficulties you were having until Mrs Clarke-Jones arrived, bursting with apology. Yet the class is over and the programme is now running to time. However did you manage?"

In the three years I had been secretary, I had not received a word of praise from the show director. Perhaps none had been deserved, but any given now would soon be retracted.

"It was quite easy," I said modestly as I lifted the escape flap in the back of the tent. "I appointed a substitute judge."

The Closing Date of Entry

As soon as I replaced the receiver the telephone shrieked again. My patience was nearly exhausted but I reminded myself that at the interview (and it seemed years instead of weeks ago) I had said that I enjoyed talking to people. It had been the truth, but talking to would-be exhibitors about late entries was quite another matter.

Wearily I lifted the receiver for the twentieth time that morning. "I'm terribly sorry," I said. "I am not allowed to take any late entries. The catalogue is with the printer. It is a society rule that all entries must be in it, otherwise the council insist that I refuse them. The closing date of entry was five days ago and the matter is now out of my hands."

By now I was like an old gramophone record, cracked but still playable. I hoped the conversation would end there but I should have known better.

"You see, I have been on holiday," a determined feminine voice said. "Not only that, but your schedule was so late in arriving that I had already missed the closing date when it came."

"We can't actually control the postal service," I pointed out, "and we do allow a few days grace; if you had returned the entry form straight away, it would probably have been all right."

"I couldn't return the entry form," she said smartly, "because there wasn't one. You forgot to enclose it."

I didn't believe it. Neither did I think it worth explaining that the packing and posting of the schedules was done by the printer.

"What is more," she added for good measure, "we have moved house and you sent the schedule to the old address, and it isn't as if we hadn't notified you. We sent you a change of address card when we paid our members' subscription, I'm sure of it."

I was equally sure she hadn't, yet I had to admire her for trotting out the stock excuses, not singly, but all together. I opened my mouth to say something but she interrupted me. "I don't see how you can possibly refuse," she said, "considering that it's your fault."

I didn't like being told it was my fault. I told her that I couldn't bend the rules, that the decisions were made by the show council, not me, and that if any of the blame *could* be attributed to me, then I was extremely sorry but there was nothing I could do.

"They are only small ponies," she said.

"They still have to be catalogued," I said.

"I could send my entry form off tonight," she said.

"I thought you hadn't received one," I said.

"I borrowed one from a friend," she said. She became distraught. "I can't miss the show," she wailed, "it's our very favourite judge; my ponies always do so well under her!"

"Then it will give the others a chance," I said.

"My husband will be furious," she cried angrily. "He will certainly cancel his show membership when I tell him how unhelpful you've been."

"I am very sorry," I said tersely, "but I cannot disobey the society rules. I can do *nothing*." She slammed down the receiver.

I stared accusingly at the show director who grinned back heartlessly over mounds of vehicle passes and admission tickets. "Twenty-one," he said, "it is a fair score, but not an all-time record. However," he added as the telephone shrilled out again, "the day is not yet over."

"Is that the show secretary?" trilled a cultured voice. "This is Lady Shildrick here, and as you know, I already have several hunters entered. However, one of the house party over the holiday would like to bring another. I'm *sure* you could just squeeze him in. I have details here if you are ready to take them down."

Mechanically, I began my speech. I had just reached the bit where the catalogue was at the printer when I realised something that made my scalp prickle.

Lady Shildrick was our landlady. The show was held on her parkland. What on earth was I saying! My speech petered out in mid-sentence. The show director, observing that my spirit had at last failed me, drew himself up and took the receiver from my grasp.

I tried to warn him but he silenced me with a majestic gesture. He took a mighty breath. "Madam," he boomed in a voice that caused a pile of numbers to slide from the table, "our entries are closed. For you, for the Queen of England, for everyone." He replaced the receiver.

I stared at him in dismay. "Whatever have you done?" I said. "I tried to tell you who it was, but you wouldn't listen."

"I neither know, nor care," he replied. "The fact remains that entries are closed. No amount of idle chatter can alter it. By the way," he added, "who was it?"

"Lady Shildrick," I said.

The show director leaned back in his chair and looked at me whilst he considered the matter. For thirty years he had been the show secretary; had sat where I sat. We were the old and the new. With the benefit of hindsight he could afford to be amused by what he saw.

"The society has a five-year contract," he said. "Only two have expired. There are still three years to run."

Yet three years in the life of an annual show were as nothing. Even with my limited experience I knew that they would pass in no time at all, and then we would be negotiating with Lady Shildrick for a renewed lease. If that lease were not renewed . . .? The prospect of having to start again elsewhere, even if elsewhere could be found, with all the impossible problems and anxiety it would entail did not bear thinking about.

"And after that?" I enquired faintly.

The show director set the jumble of show-jumping numbers back on the table. "After that," he said, "I shall have retired."

A Grand Parade

"How many admission tickets are allowed per animal?" I asked the show director. He made no reply, being engrossed in unpacking returned trophies, the Insurance Claim File already open on his desk.

I repeated the question in a somewhat louder tone of voice. "What's the animal?" he said absently, adding in a grievous voice, "Oh, my giddy Aunt, half a page of the *Sun* and they consider it securely packed. Just look at this!" He held up a solid, silver cup newly decorated with several deep scratches, a large dent and a handle bent to forty-five degrees. "I can't understand the mentality of some people," he said sadly. "Not even a *with care* or a *fragile*."

I commiserated. "How many admission tickets per animal?" I repeated. "A pony. Trout Hill Riding School."

"Naturally, I shall be unable to claim recompense from the post office. They will only shriek insufficient postage, and who could argue?"

"Who indeed?" I agreed. "But how many . . ."

"One pony, one ticket," the show director said, drawing out a pink claim form. "Unless they specifically ask for two. How many does he ask for?"

"Four," I said.

"Four?"

"Four. One for the rider, one for the attendant because it's the leading-rein class, one for the owner and one for the driver."

"Good Lord. They have got it down to a fine art." The show director's voice was not without a tinge of admiration.

"But how many shall I send? A simple answer to a simple question is all that I ask."

"Do I detect a trace of irritation? It is no matter for whom the extra tickets are requested. Be it the Prime Minister or the Pope. One pony, one ticket. Unless they specifically ask for two."

"They asked for four."

"They did." The director's hand flew down the claim form, describing, deleting, assessing the damage.

"l shall resign," I said. "I shall do it at once. I resign here and now; I shall put it in writing." I reached for a pen.

The show director chortled with amusement. "Give him two tickets; and while I think of it, ignore the entry from Cowslip Farm, name of Brown. Put it straight into the waste bin. Pretend you never received it."

I sighed. "Yesterday the information would have been of value; today it is of no use. The tickets and labels went off last night. The society rules that all entries accompanied by the correct fees must be accepted so you can hardly blame me; anyway, why ignore it? What's wrong with his entry?"

"What was the entry this time? Shire horse? Ram? Dairy short-horn?"

"Sow and litter," I said.

The director nodded. "At two pounds an entry, it's still a cheap way of bringing in one's friends and relations."

"Oh no," I said, "not really." I hid a smile, thinking of Mr Brown's friends and relations making noises like a sow and litter as the cattle waggon rolled through the exhibitors' entrance.

The show director looked up. Little escaped him. Behind him was a lifetime of experience detecting insincerity. He pointed his pen at me in a solemn manner. "You will stop Mr Brown," he said, yet a gleam of amusement lit his eye as he returned his attentions to the claim form. "But next year," he added.

It was early, if any time could be said to be early on a show day. The word tends to lose its meaning when nobody sleeps.

The bars and the catering marquees were still un-opened. The avenues between the trade stands were blocked with delivery vans. The general public were just a mere trickle through the turnstiles and the press tent was empty. From the collecting ring behind my tent came the regular thud of hooves; the first hunter class was just coming out of the ring. I sat with a blank result sheet in front of me, waiting for the ring steward to bring me the placings.

A shadow fell across my desk. It was not the ring steward, it was an exhibitor; her badge proclaimed it. She was a large woman and she wore a mackintosh and a head scarf, although it was not raining. She flourished a catalogue. She looked belligerent.

"Good morning," I said.

"I want to see the secretary," she demanded.

"That's me," I said, pointing to my badge. The society ruled that we change the colour of every badge each year. Thus they hoped to thwart those who imagined they could gain admission by using the same one twice. We were running out of colours. This year's colour for my badge was pale lilac and it was attached to an even paler ribbon. It was silver blocked with *Secretary* if you looked close enough; but it was not a badge to command respect, it was defensive, apologetic even.

My early visitor was unimpressed. She rested her hands on my table and stared at me. "This grand parade," she said grimly, and my heart sank. "Am I to understand that unless I parade my exhibit at 4.30 this afternoon, I lose my prize money?"

"You do," I said.

She flung her catalogue onto the table and made a great display of looking at her watch. "It is now 9.15 exactly," she said. "What do you suggest I do for the next seven hours?"

I sighed. I had had the same argument myself, but as an exhibitor, and from her side of the table. The show secretaries had found small consolation for me either.

"It does seem harsh, I admit," I agreed. "But it is a society rule and it is my job to see that the rules are not broken."

She drew herself up suddenly, I drew back, not quite knowing what was going to happen next, but she had spotted the show director entering through the back of the tent. She abandoned me at once. She turned to the show director and she brightened visibly; her expression clearly said that here is someone with superior intellect, someone with whom I can converse On My Own Level.

The show director beamed. "Good Morning, madam," he said. His badge was gold blocked on navy blue.

The ring steward was a welcome sight. "Results of class one for you, miss," he said, handing me the sheet. "Knew you'd have trouble with that one," he said, nodding towards the show director who appeared to be commiserating with the exhibitor upon the injustices of life. "She had a go at us first. Go and see the secretary, we told her, she'll sort you out." He banged his bowler hat back on to his head and went back towards the main ring.

I heard the show director say, "Yet if we bend the rules for one, we shall be expected to do it for all; the Grand Parade of Prizewinners is the highlight of the show. The public pay to see it, they expect it, and without their money we could not stage the show."

The irate exhibitor was forced to agree that the public were entitled to see fair return for their money. On the other hand she had a vet coming out to see one of her horses after lunch. What was he going to say when there was nobody at home? Who was going to pay the call-out fee?

The show director agreed that it was unfortunate. "Use my telephone," he suggested, "and put him off until tomorrow."

He placed the receiver in her hands and jiggled the button that called the local exchange on our temporary line. The exhibitor, at first doubtful, finally beamed back at him and asked for the number she wanted. I heaved a sigh of relief.

The show director sailed out of the tent, barely closing one eye as he passed my table. He almost collided with a small, cross-looking person in a tweed suit who was just on her way in.

"Madam, I do beg your pardon," he said graciously, whilst making a swift exit.

The small, cross-looking person came up to my table and squinted at my badge. She leaned over the award sheets and stared at me angrily. "Now, secretary," she said. "What's all this about having to stay for the grand parade?"

Hunter Trials and Tribulations

The initial meeting to discuss the forthcoming hunter trials was, if only we had realised it, an omen of future disaster.

Most of the committee arrived at the appointed hour; the stragglers drifted in, with the notable exception of the Hunt Supporters' Club chairman. Hasty telephone calls to his home discovered him in the bath. "What meeting?" he enquired in heated tones when he was called to the telephone, dripping water onto the parquet.

"I sent you a card, I sent everybody one," the secretary told him.

"Well, I never received it!" he shouted.

"You did! You did!" cried the secretary. "I posted them all myself; everybody had one!"

"Stop this hullabaloo, somebody," the district commissioner said wearily.

The master took the telephone receiver out of the secretary's hand. "We will give you fifteen minutes," he said tersely. The Hunt Club chairman was with us in ten.

One of the local landowners had finally been persuaded, after much discussion and with deep reluctance, to allow his parkland to be used as a venue. The master was adamant that the course should make the most of the natural resources, the park having a goodly footage of post and rail, hedges, a stream, a small pond and an abundance of fallen tree trunks.

Mr Trimbee, who had been appointed course builder in chief, didn't like the sound of it. The previous year he had been to Chatsworth Horse Trials and had become quite carried away with visions of log tables, tractor tyres, and Helsinki steps.

"Hardly the kind of obstacle one would expect to meet when hounds were running," observed the master, dryly.

The course builder in chief accused the committee of lack of imagination.

"But this is hunter trials, not Olympic eventing," the pony club secretary pointed out.

The course builder was affronted. He said that if anybody thought he was going to spend his precious time trimming hedges and sewing flags, he would resign. He could think of better things to do. He thumped on the table and upset a glass of water over the hunt secretary's notes.

"Restrain him, somebody," the district commissioner said in a tired voice. He never lifted a finger himself, but several years as a commissioned officer had made him a master of delegation.

The Hunt Club chairman commented that as a meeting it was hardly worth getting out of the bath for. This reminded the secretary that he had said he had not received a notification. Several arguments were now going on at once. The hunt secretary, who had been trying to take the minutes, threw down her pen and walked out.

The meeting ended in uproar. The landowner's agent, who had sat speechless throughout, rushed back to his employer full of reassurances. There was absolutely no need for concern, he told him, the event would never take place. The hunt committee were totally incapable of organising anything whatsoever; the hunter trials would never get off the ground. The following week the course builder and his men moved into the park to start building the course.

When the course was completed, everyone was forced to agree that the course builder in chief had done a magnificent job. Most of the fences had an 'A', 'B', or 'C' section. The 'C's were fairly easy, the 'B's difficult, and the 'A's horrific. The hedges were beautifully laid, the post and rails were solid and inviting, the gates had been freshly creosoted. A tiger trap and a moderate bank with a drop fence on the landing side had been constructed in the open parkland, as had the zig-zag obstacle of birch poles. There was an interesting sheep pen affair in the thicket; the pond could be cleared easily by a horse and there was a single rail set a stride away from the bank. Small ponies could paddle across as the depth was only ten inches and the bottom was firm.

The obstacle that was the course builder's pride and joy was the stream. He had faced each bank with railway sleepers and horses were to jump down the bank into the stream, take two or three strides in the water and hurl themselves back onto dry land. It was a miracle of construction and ingenuity and the course builder was justly proud of it. "Almost as good as Burghley," he boasted.

His next task was to construct a tower for the commentators, to enable them to view the course in its entirety. The soaring construction of poles and planks looked somewhat precarious. The top of the platform was protected by a tarpaulin, and a table and two chairs had been securely nailed to the floor. The course builder demonstrated how they should ascend by rope-ladder; scotch and sandwiches could be hauled up by means of a pulley operated from the ground.

"Is it safe?" one of the commentators enquired nervously.

The course builder cried that it was as safe as anything could possibly be. Why, hadn't it taken three whole days to construct? Didn't it even have a roof to protect them from the elements? Was not everything arranged with their convenience and comfort in mind?

The commentators shaded their eyes and gazed up at their ideal home for the duration of the hunter trials. It swayed gently in the wind. They exchanged apprehensive glances.

The Hunt Club chairman was elected to test the course so that a time could be set and also to ascertain that the magnificent fences were actually jumpable. His horse was aged and disliked jumping at speed and in cold blood. The old horse cantered reluctantly through the start and laboured up the incline towards the first jump, but when he saw the newly laid hedge in front of him he stopped dead. The Hunt Club chairman flew onwards alone and vanished from sight. Everyone groaned but it was only a hint of things to come. The horse stopped at least three times at every obstacle. The time-keeper clicked away at his stop-watch and looked harassed.

The fifth obstacle was the pen in the thicket. The horse refused the first part once then sailed through; the effect was partially ruined by the Hunt Club chairman being swept out of the saddle over the second part by some overhanging branches nobody had considered. Screams of pain accompanied their sixth and finally successful attempt to negotiate the bullfinch. The course builder, short of birch, admitted that it was made of blackthorn.

When the old horse reached the pond he really dug his toes in. Eventually the Hunt Club chairman lost his temper and galloped him at it flat out. The old horse, determined not to jump it, applied his brakes too late and was forced to take off, landing in the middle of the

". . . don't just stand there!"

pond with a tremendous splash. Cascades of spray flew into the air soaking the master and the time-keeper and causing the course builder to cry out with rage. There had been little enough water in the pond to start with, he cried, now the steaming idiot had emptied it.

The Hunt Club chairman tried the same galloping tactics at the stream. The old horse appeared to fall off the sleeper-faced bank and failed to reappear. Those who were on foot stood on the top of the bank and looked down; the banks were three feet high and sheer. The Hunt Club chairman and the old horse looked up at those on the bank. "Well don't just *stand* there," the chairman said angrily. "DO something!"

"What would you like us to do?" the pony club secretary said helpfully, "fetch a crane? Or a tow rope?"

"Let him stay there," the course builder said vengefully, "spoiling my take-offs. Emptying my pond."

"I give up," the time-keeper said. "How can I set a time? It's taken him an hour and four minutes to get this far!"

"Get him out, somebody," the district commissioner said. "Before he drowns."

The pony club secretary delivered a sound whack to the rump of the chairman's horse with a long stick. Startled, it leapt up the bank with the chairman clinging round its neck and, reaching dry land, dropped its head and deposited him on the grass.

"Twenty-three refusals and eight falls so far," said the hunt secretary who had been keeping count. "It must be some kind of record."

"He'll have to go round again," the district commissioner decided. "We can't set a time like this. Tell him, somebody."

The day of the hunter trials dawned. The hunt committee had never seen rain like it. It absolutely bucketed down. The pond overflowed and the stream became a yellow, gushing torrent. Competitors struggling to walk the course returned to their horse boxes muttering that the fences were worse than one would expect to find at Badminton.

The secretary sat in her caravan with the rain drumming on the roof and wrote out a sign to put in her window. CANCELLATIONS ACCEPTED WITH PLEASURE it read, adding at the treasurer's insistence, *BUT NO ENTRY FEES REFUNDED.*

All over the course the jump judges stood dismally under golf umbrellas, their flags and their score sheets soaked and their scores illegible because their ballpoint pens refused to write. The commentators cried that their eyrie leaked abominably and sent out urgent messages for mackintoshes and more scotch.

Competitors who braved the course were sent out at ten minute intervals, but there were so many refusals that there were long queues at every jump. They cantered through the finish in threes and fours, sending up showers of spray and blinding the time-keeper who was on the verge of mental collapse.

Lemon breeches and smart jackets or cross-country jerseys with silk covered hats returned through the finish a uniform mud colour, as did the horses and ponies. Parents had great difficulty in identifying their offspring. "It's Sarah!" they cried, adding on closer inspection, "No it isn't, it's Godfrey."

So many riders ended up flying solo over the sleeper-faced bank into the brook that the jump judge was reinforced with a member of the St. John's Ambulance brigade well-versed in artificial respiration. Nobody knew what the results were because the outside blackboard was washed clean every time anyone attempted to post the scores on it. The secretary's caravan was bursting at the seams with sodden competitors demanding to know where they had finished and it was only as she struggled out to get the results broadcast by the commentators that she noticed their tower was leaning at a perilous angle. An urgent message was sent up via the pulley, followed by a swift evacuation just before the ideal home crashed to the ground. The commentators were out for the course builder's blood. "We could have been killed!" they cried. "Where is the varmint?"

"In the bar," the secretary said. "With the master, the chairman, the district commissioner and all others of sound mind."

In the midst of the coughs and sniffles of the following committee meeting it was reported that there had been no serious casualties apart from a few thorns acquired at the bullfinch, some severe chills and not a few hangovers. However, the treasurer reported, the hunter trials had not been a financial success; in fact the only people who had made any money had been the local farmers who had lined up their tractors by the gates towards the end of the day bearing placards proclaiming TOW YOU OUT FOR A POUND.

The course builder just couldn't believe it. "Do you mean that after all that work, all that *effort*, we didn't make any profit at *all*?" he said.

The treasurer replied that after all expenses had been paid there had actually been a very small profit at the end of the day, which in the circumstances, must be regarded as little short of a miracle.

The Hunt Supporters' Club chairman demanded to know the extent of the miracle in the form of hard cash.

The treasurer estimated it at approximately sixty pounds.

It was at this point that the landowner's agent rose and presented the treasurer with a bill for reseeding the park. It came to sixty pounds exactly.

To Swell the Hunt Club Funds

Late spring. The Farmers' Hunt and the Hunt Ball proper were over, as was the Point-to-Point. Hunting memories receded, fences were repaired, irate land-owners were pacified, one Siamese cat was replaced. Two divorces were well under way. The Hunt Supporters' Club turned in anticipation to their treasurer. He, in the manner of all treasurers, had been appointed to the position not because of any financial acumen, but on the strength of his doleful countenance and pessimistic nature. "Not a man," the district commissioner had said, "to be carried away by foolish and extravagant suggestions. Elect him, somebody."

The committee met in a burst of ill-founded optimism. Was there enough in the kitty to cover the cost of the proposed extension to the kennels? To re-fence the hound exercise yard? To fit a new container body to the horse box? Their imaginations ran riot. In their mind's eye their collected wealth assumed gigantic proportions. The Hunt Club chairman became positively animated. The master's face assumed a glazed expression.

The treasurer rose to his feet. He held up a hand in a weary gesture and heaved a long and gusty sigh. Speculation immediately ceased. Every face around the table assumed an anxious aspect and a pall of apprehension descended.

The treasurer said that, taking into consideration the disastrous hunter trials, the provision of a new hound trailer, the necessary purchase of a duplicator for the secretary, the lamentable absence of enthusiasm over capping (by collectors and car-followers alike), and the unbelievable reluctance of members to pay their subscriptions promptly, the resultant monies reposing in the current bank account were not sufficient to buy a hamster cage.

Thus said, the treasurer sat. The master let out a low whistle from between his teeth. The chairman humped up his shoulders and tucked in his chin like a hibernating tortoise. For a moment everyone looked dazed.

The district commissioner took control. He assumed a commanding air. "We shall have to rectify the situation," he said in a positive tone.

"We?" the Hunt Club chairman said in faint surprise, but the district commissioner was immune to sarcasm.

"Has anyone any suggestions?" he asked hopefully.

"It was once suggested," the secretary said, "that we hold a Pony Club ball."

"Too expensive," the treasurer said.

"Too complicated," the chairman said.

"And too bloody noisy," the master added.

The secretary said that the occasion need be none of these things. A band was not necessary for the young people of today, they preferred a discotheque which need cost no more than forty pounds. The treasurer immediately looked interested. Elaborate food was not necessary either, hot dogs and jacket potatoes were the thing to have and they were very cheap. As for drinks, fruit cups and cider-based punches would suffice. It was a well-known fact that the Quorn had made seven hundred and fifty pounds profit on their Pony Club Ball.

"Sounds a good idea," the district commissioner said at once. "Go ahead."

There were murmurs of interest and agreement. The only difficulty the secretary could see, was going to be where to hold the ball; it couldn't possibly be held in a village hall; the Pony Club members were the subscribers of the future and the setting was of vital importance. The venue must definitely have some social cachet.

The master groaned. His residence had accommodated both the farmers' hunt and the hunt ball proper. Of all the big houses in the country, it was the only one to boast a ballroom and facilities for a gathering of any magnitude. As faces around the table turned towards him with ingratiating beams he raised his hands in a gesture of resignation. He was defeated and he knew it.

The ball was a sell out. Six hundred tickets were printed and the whole lot were spoken for within two weeks. The reason for the phenomenal success was simple. The Pony Club members sent in their ticket applications. Doubtful parents, remembering the hunt balls of their youth, decided they should not be unchaperoned, and applied for tickets themselves. In order not to appear unsporting, they hunted out cousins of the appropriate age whose parents came as company for the others. In no time at all it had turned into a family gathering; a positive host, a veritable multitude of relatives accompanied the Pony Club members to witness, with wonder, their offspring at their first ball; to recapture, misty-eyed, the enchantment of their lost youth. Or so they thought.

Whilst the Pony Club members scowled and sulked over the promised orgy that was clearly destined not to take place; whilst parents fussed over plum velvet dinner jackets and ruffled shirts, worried about the suitability of startling garments by Zandra Rhodes, whilst grannies hunted out their shawls and draw-string dorothy bags, the committee rubbed their hands with glee.

Even the treasurer was smiling. "Everything will be most satisfactory," he declared. "Providing that there is no damage."

"Damage?" enquired the chairman scornfully. "What damage could there possibly be?" He reminded the treasurer that in three hunt farmers' balls, three hunt balls proper, and five cheese and wine parties, the only casualties had been a few broken glasses and the master's reproduction statue of Adonis which someone had reversed into by mistake. "Damage," he snorted to himself. "Fiddlesticks!"

Three hours prior to the commencement of the ball found most of the committee in the nether regions of the kitchens mixing fruit cups in a selection of plastic dustbins. The secretary went upstairs and, when she had labelled the ladies' and gents' cloakrooms, went up and down the landings, locking all the bedroom doors and pocketing the keys. The master watched this performance in some alarm. "Fire precautions," the secretary said comfortingly.

In the ballroom the regiment of long mullioned windows had been effectively blacked out. Three persons of indeterminate sex were setting up a selection of revolving, flashing multi-coloured lights and a projector which threw Popeye films onto an adjacent wall.

When the amplifiers were tested the entire feline population of the house (which was considerable) leapt simultaneously into the air and fled at high speed. The master grew pale and gazed apprehensively at his costly collection of antique porcelain.

The chairman had elected himself chief taster of the cider-based fruit cup and the slightly more potent variety considered suitable for the adults. After an hour or so his cheeks became less rosy and more pea-green. He grew belligerent when someone suggested he desist from further sampling. Comments on his pallor he interpreted as aspersions upon his drinking capacity. "Are you insinuating I can't hold my liquor?" he shouted at the treasurer, whose waterproof clothing had been designed for wading in the Spey. The treasurer emptied another bottle of amber liquid and stirred the contents of his dustbin vigorously with a broom handle. He plunged a glass into it and proffered it to the chairman, holding it up to the light in admiration. "Beautiful," he said, "try it." The chairman made no reply; instead he clutched the kitchen table and then made a rapid exit via the back door. The treasurer hooted with laughter and downed the glass of fruit cup himself; after which he made a wry face and

. . . the Pony Club members did not enjoy their ball

peered unhappily into the murky depths of his dustbin.

It is fair to say that the Pony Club members did not enjoy their ball. They disliked the fruit cup intensely. "Where is the Martini?" they cried, "the Bacardi and the Champers?" They regarded the hot dogs and jacket potatoes with distaste. "How *common*," they said. "How uncivilised." "Think thin, Victoria, imagine the *calories*!" Whilst their parents queued up for the hot dogs, "Such a refreshing change, kedgeree does get *boring* after a while, don't you think?" whilst their aunts and uncles leapt about in the discotheque, "Super fun! Never had anything like this in our day!" whilst their grannies sipped the fruit cup, "So good for one. The vitamins you know," the Pony Club members wandered about, bored and distracted.

They amused themselves by reading their host's correspondence in his study. They receipted his unpaid bills and transferred them to the 'out' basket. They wandered round the kitchens and made themselves Stilton sandwiches and instant coffee. Somebody found half a dustbin of discarded fruit cup and poured a wineglass-full into every wellington boot in the scullery. Others searched the library shelves for erotica and, disappointed, spent the evening inking in the 'o's' in a rare first edition with the master's quill and inkpot.

In the early hours of the morning, one of the girls complained that the small sitting room in which a group had secreted themselves was becoming chilly. One of the young men put a match to the decorative arrangement of logs and crepe paper in the fireplace. All were blissfully unaware that the chimney had been well stuffed with fertilizer bags to prevent a down draught. Finding the ensuing smoke distasteful, they abandoned the room. They closed the door.

The unisex disc jockey was just announcing the last record before the end of the ball when the chimney erupted with a mighty roar.

The Hunt Club funds are healthy again, as is the chairman. The master regained his temper when the new fencing round the hound exercise yard was erected. The district commissioner appeared when it was all over and said, "Surprising what a joint effort can achieve, you know. When we all pull together."

The parents and grand-parents declared it the best ball they had ever attended, but the Pony Club threatened to disband if anyone ever organised another; and as for the Fire Brigade, after being initially taken aback by the height and the size of the chimney, why, they were positively enchanted by the whole affair.

D'YE KEN MRS AKRILL . . .

My spell as a hunting correspondent was short-lived and traumatic, but as I am an indifferent rider and an inveterate coward to boot, it was generally considered a miracle that I managed to survive two seasons with the Puckeridge and Thurlow; not perhaps one of the fastest or most fashionable packs, but certainly as far as I was concerned, one of the most hospitable, friendly and tolerant.

The pilot article for the hunting diary series was the result of a day out cubbing with the terrier-men of the hunt. I was bundled into the back of a tiny Renault with three men, four terriers in stout wire cages, an assortment of spades and two huge signs which said, "Danger! Animals on the Road!" It was murder. I sat on a tin ledge five inches wide; the signs crashed up and down; the spades flew. I clung onto the terrier cages. The terrier-men looked at me gleefully. "Watch out for your fingers," they said, "they're a bit sharp."

We followed hounds across country, down cart tracks, up hills, over clover and acres of burnt stubble, leaping the plough which saved the few hedges from the flames of a spent harvest. If there was doubt about whether the undergrowth disguised a ditch, we took a running dive at it; the Renault flew over. At the end of it all, the master, in recognition of my journalistic bravery, presented me with a brush. I was hooked.

My editor, Michael Williams of *Light Horse*, signed off his letter acknowledging receipt of the first instalment with ". . . and I only hope that you won't land me with any libel action." But rather to his surprise, I fancy, neither the hunt, nor my hunting friends, Elaine and Glynis (who have found themselves endlessly lampooned both in the diary and elsewhere), ever uttered a word of complaint; even Moss

Bros., having followed the continuing saga of the full hunt coat with glee, professed themselves well pleased and took out larger advertising space on the strength of it; thus proving themselves sporting tailors in more ways than hitherto realised.

My first season was both frightening and exorbitantly expensive, involving the purchase of a horse, saddlery, a trailer, hunting clothes, and the payment of a stiff hunt subscription. By the time my hunter had been rolled over by a car (a dramatic experience related here as it appeared in the Hunting Diary, and also capitalised upon as fiction in *A Hoof in the Door*), which necessitated the purchase of another, I was already sadly out of pocket.

My seasons were also the wettest on record. I stood dismally outside the dripping coverts in my sodden (and by the end, it has to be said, shrunken) full hunt coat, squelched along the rides under leaden skies, slithered perilously down the sides of ditches that gushed and roared, and toiled over acres of sticky plough that pulled off my horse's shoes with appalling regularity and strained his joints so that it looked as if someone had been round his legs with a bicycle pump.

In my two seasons I saw enough of hunting (not to mention blacksmiths and veterinary surgeons) to last me a lifetime and, as a result, I must be one of the few people alive who can watch the hunt go by with pleasure, but entirely without envy.

No Thoroughbreds Need Apply

"Hunting," my husband said, the word accompanied by a hollow little laugh, "is for the brave. Think of the flying fences, the yawning ditches. Imagine the galloping, iron-shod hooves, the cries of the wounded. Consider all of this, and then stick to showing ponies."

"Showing ponies is a summer occupation," I said.

My husband lifted his eyes from the perplexity of the profit and loss accounts. "In order to hunt," he said severely, "one would require a horse, a subscription, specific items of clothing and," he hinted darkly, "countless other things."

"They needn't be new," I said.

For just one moment there was silence, then, "A horse," he replied in the tone of one who happily swims only to realise the tide has turned against him, "is *always* new."

I spent a long time composing the advertisement. After all, I was certainly not one of the brave. Not for me the headlong gallop of the thruster, the burning ambition to be amongst the first flight; not for me the chronicled feats of the Empress of Austria or Lucy Glitters; I only wanted to tootle.

In truth, the thought of bestriding a mettlesome, thoroughbred hunter, its massive heart swelled with courage, its powerful shoulders flecked with foam, its beautiful legs strung with tendons like iron bands made me feel very nervous indeed. I didn't want a thoroughbred with scope and speed, what I wanted was a small, stout animal, short of stride and placid of temperament. All I wanted was enough action to keep my circulation working. I saw myself traversing the lanes at a spanking trot, cantering briskly across the stubble fields and hopping over a conveniently small log. These modest pleasure were all I desired from the chase: essentially I needed a mount of the same mind.

The finished advertisement read: *Pretty cob required, suitable for lightweight neurotic to hunt*. I was proud of this witty and truthful little advertisement but to be honest, I was not altogether sure what a pretty cob was. To judge by the replies I received, neither was anyone else.

The owner of the first animal I went to see regarded me with delight. "Oh, he'll be just super for you!" she cried in ringing Pony Club tones. "He'll be absolutely perfect!"

The 'super' article she produced was a pony, narrow chested and roan and thirteen hands high. It stood to attention with its boxy feet together and looked surprised to be presented with such dash and ceremony. I patted its hogged, upside-down neck and thanked the owner for her trouble but regretted that it was a little too small.

The next offering was a fifteen hand cob. He was exactly the right size, type and temperament, but he was piebald with a wall eye and a pink corrugated nose like a pig. All of this might have been endured but when standing at ease he had the distressing habit of unrolling his sheath. Under delicate questioning his owner maintained that this was but a manifestation of his extremely relaxed and placid temperament. I was impressed by this explanation but at the same time I could see that there would be certain disadvantages in owning a horse with such a habit especially when hunting, which involved much standing about at the covert-side, and at the meet which might provide ample opportunity for relaxation of an embarrassing nature; one's friends and acquaintances would try not to notice, but their eyes would be drawn all the same. I explained to the owner that, not wanting to draw undue attention to myself in the hunting field, I was unable to buy a horse that was piebald.

My next expedition was to inspect a cob who would have been ideal were it not for the fact that it almost coughed me out of the saddle whilst its eyes ran like twin water-spouts. "It's hay fever," its owner said apologetically. "It's his only fault, he's allergic to it."

I was summoned to a riding school whose proprietor cried, "Bring out Goliath!" and displayed for my admiration a monstrous beast of eighteen hands high accompanied by a kitchen chair in order that I might reach the stirrup. Goliath slid his feet along the tarmac as if shod with saucepan lids and when he trotted he tripped. I found this a hideously alarming experience and said so. "It's only because he needs shoeing," the proprietor assured me, "It must be all of two weeks since he was last shod."

I went to see subsequent animals too strong, too impossibly ugly, who refused to go, who refused to stop, who had only one good leg out of four, all of whom were rather more money than my budget had allowed for and only most regretfully for sale.

I became disheartened. I abandoned the replies to my own clever little advertisement and began to pay attention to those composed by other people. I set out to investigate one of them. *Six-year-old gelding, quiet and well-mannered, hunted two seasons.*

When I arrived I saw that he was not what I wanted at all. He was too big (sixteen hands) and too expensive (six hundred pounds) and he was a thoroughbred. Worse, he was a chestnut thoroughbred with three long white socks. He was not even pretty, having a goose rump, no bone to speak of, and lop ears; yet he had a certain picturesque quality as he trotted round the paddock, dishing vigorously with his near fore, and a prodigiously affable manner in the stable.

His owner, after several revolutions of the paddock the better to display his long-striding if somewhat indirect paces, enquired if I would care to take the saddle, and having observed no inclination on the horse's part to buck, rear, bolt or indulge in any such anti-social behaviour, I accepted.

The saddle, being a Stübben of the most costly variety, was very comfortable with a welcoming dip in the middle and voluptuous knee and thigh rolls. Sitting in it, embraced by it, I dared to feel nearly confident. I walked and trotted and cantered the chestnut and almost, but not quite, attempted a gallop. The owner, seeing that everything was going well, dispatched me towards the main road to test for myself the horse's reputation for total reliability in traffic. Through the town centre we progressed, weaving our way through cars and bicycles, overtaken by milk floats, negotiating lorries and pedestrians with never a twitch of the lop ears. It was all simply wonderful, and as we clopped past Sainsbury's and I caught a glimpse of our reflection in the plate glass window, I was terribly, overwhelmingly, impressed with what I saw. Why, mounted upon the chestnut horse, seated upon the Stübben saddle, I was almost a horsewoman.

I dismissed there and then all my inhibitions about thoroughbreds and chestnuts and white socks. I bought him.

A Full Hunt Coat

I was going to Bernard Weatherill but the taxi driver couldn't find it.

"No matter," I said grandly, as we entered Savile Row for the third time. "We shall go to Moss instead."

"Moss Bros.," he said, "is Covent Garden. It is on the *other side*."

He peered at me through the partition as if in doubt that my person could withstand such an extravagant journey.

Moss Bros. welcomed me, if not with open arms, with genial approbation. If they hated my too-tight jeans, if they loathed my Fenwicks shirt made in Hong Kong, they hid it well. In their bespoke department they flourished their swatches, waved their tape measures and called out to each other measurements which sounded disagreeably large.

My own assistant was tall and stooped and weary and spoke with an Irish accent. "Will ye be wantin' the full hunt coat, m'am?"

I would indeed, but as a matter of interest, I would like to know the price. For one brief moment my assistant looked disconcerted. He produced a large book of prices and turned its pages and sighed a great deal over the figures. Clearly it had been tiresome of me to enquire.

. . . they flourished their swatches and waved their tape measures

"The full hunt coat," he said, with just a touch of grandeur, "Will be costing you one hundred and forty-six pounds. And," he added, in a voice that held a promise of delights in store, "we will be calling you in time for your fitting."

Eight weeks went by with nobody from Moss Bros. calling me at all. I hastened up to the city, slipping into Herbert Johnson to be measured for a hat. The purchase of a hat for hunting is fraught with anxiety beset on one side by the rules of etiquette and tradition and on the other by personal preference and the wish to preserve one's skull intact. The bowler hat is strictly correct wear for hunting ladies, but it is neither as becoming nor as safe as the velvet cap. The hunt secretary was no help. In answer to my enquiry upon this delicate matter he was cautious and evasive. If I already possessed a velvet cap, the hunt would not like me to embark upon any additional expense on their behalf; at the same time I should realise that velvet caps were the prerogative of hunt servants and farmers, and I was neither. This was undoubtedly true, but as I valued my skull every bit as highly as theirs, I decided to have a velvet cap and hang the consequences; vanity also had something to do with the decision.

A suave gentleman assistant in Herbert Johnson's placed several hats upon my head and all were an alarming shade of burgundy. Observing my look of wonder, he said, "Disregard the colour, if you will, m'am, and concentrate upon the style." But I was thrown completely by his next offering, which was in spring cabbage green.

Further up Bond Street, I had a fancy to have my boots made by Maxwell, bootmaker to the very best people.

When it was my turn to be measured I was ushered into a curtained alcove and seated upon what appeared to be a faded throne on a dais.

"I would like a pair of boots for hunting," I said.

The face that hovered on a level with my knees said, "Waxed calf boots, m'am, will be twelve months."

I said I couldn't wait that long, what about box calf.

The face assumed an expression of grave offence. "Box calf, m'am, are unsuitable for hunting. If Maxwells make your hunting boots they will be made of waxed calf."

"But how long would it take to make them from box calf?" I insisted.

"Relatively quickly," he said.

"How quickly?"

"Six months."

In the shoe department at Moss Bros. I found a sympathetic assistant who produced a vast array of box calf hunting boots within the space of a few minutes. I stumped up and down in boots longer and shorter, wider and narrower, past nattily suited gentlemen selecting new shoes for the office who exchanged nervous glances. Ready-mades are not at all like hand-made waxed calf shaped to one's own leg, being stiff and hard and distressingly wide around the ankles. However, I found some that were generally agreed to be a good fit – as much as one is able to judge when one's upper limbs are clad in a flowered skirt.

In the bespoke department, my assistant was sighing over a ledger. He looked at me without recognition. I told him about my eight weeks and nobody calling.

"Eight weeks," he said. "Glory! By what name would you be calling yourself, m'am?"

He looked me up in an order book and vanished into a room behind the cubicles.

"Would it be a side-saddle skirt you wanted?" he called.

"No," I said.

"No," he agreed, "it wouldn't. It hasn't the name on it. Ah!" he exclaimed, and after a pregnant interval, emerged with a pair of khaki breeches.

"They are not mine," I said.

He looked at the work label. "They are indeed," he said triumphantly. "They've your own name on them."

"They are not mine," I said firmly. "Not that colour. Not brown breeches for hunting. I ordered cream."

"We don't make cream britches," he said.

"You do," I said. I was beginning to panic.

"We don't."

"I want to see the swatches," I said. I wondered if I should jump out of the window.

He produced them, the light of battle in his eye. I pointed to the colour I had ordered.

"That's not cream at all," he said. "That's white."

"It looks like cream," I said.

"Fancy that now," he said, "a lady who doesn't know cream from white."

"They are still the wrong colour," I said. "White breeches are not khaki breeches."

"Then you'll have made a mistake when you placed the order," he said. He returned to the order book and after a moment's absorption, he peered over the till. "I can now reveal to you," he said slowly, "that you did indeed order white britches!" And he slammed the book down on the counter and made me jump.

"Where is the full hunt coat?" I asked faintly.

"M'am, I have not the vaguest notion," he said. He looked as if he might weep.

Urgent calling upon the intercom produced, after a goodly interval, the fitter, who was forced to admit that the full hunt coat had not yet been started. "However," he said brightly, "as we have the breeches, albeit in the wrong colour, we may as well try them on for size."

I agreed, but with an air of resignation which I hoped would suggest that perhaps Moss Bros. was not what one had been led to believe.

The breeches stopped my circulation below the knee. "They are too tight," I said.

The fitter agreed that they were; that also the waistband was too loose and the calves too slack. All these things, he said, would have to be put right and the breeches re-made in the correct shade. It would take no time at all.

When he had managed to separate them from my knees he went off with them over his arm. The khaki breeches were delicately patterned with chalk marks.

"And how would they be for m'am?" my assistant asked the fitter as he passed the counter.

"Perfect," he said.

A New Subscriber

Speeding into Moss Bros. a week before the opening meet to collect the full hunt coat, my eye alighted upon my breeches. Would I need to try them on, I wondered?

The bespoke assistant smiled winningly. Surely they would be perfect for ma'am by now? Hadn't they been made and re-made, altered and re-altered to accommodate me? Surely this time they would be fitting like the proverbial glove.

Ringing him the following day to explain how their seat hung four inches below mine and the buttons began their descent on the point of my knee, I said: "The full hunt coat is perfection, but the breeches will be the most famous of your disasters." Not one whit disturbed by this, the bespoke assistant thanked me profusely and wished me an enjoyable season. I went to my local saddlers and bought a pair of two-way stretch ready-mades. They looked and felt like ballet tights.

After this there was the blacksmith; or to be completely accurate, there wasn't the blacksmith. When he had failed to keep the fourth appointment I was about to answer an advertisement for a do-it-yourself shoeing kit with explanatory leaflet entitled 'Be Your Own Blacksmith', when the most incredible racket started up in the stable yard. Investigation revealed a mini pick-up upon which a mobile forge roared and cranked and bellowed smoke, all of which was outdone by a transistor radio at full throat; and in the midst of all this, two long-haired, male persons were shoeing my horse.

After years of nursing aged and grumbling blacksmiths forever threatening retirement, the travelling discotheque was a wondrous event and my horse was shod within half an hour. All was now ready for the opening meet, or would have been had I not decided to clip.

My horse hadn't been clipped before, but he didn't mind; he stood as if hewn from rock until I ran the clippers up his face. He didn't like it. He leapt in the air and the performance that followed left me in no doubt that was the end of the clipping as far as he was concerned. From opposite ends of the stable we regarded each other with mutual distrust; the chestnut looked like a panda with great rings left round his eyes and dramatic zig-zags at the top of his neck. In other circumstances I might have laughed, but I thought of the full hunt coat and the paid-up subscription and I felt rather desperate.

I transported my handiwork to a local stable that boasted a man who could clip anything. My poor chestnut, grabbed by his lop ears, twitched by his nose, did his very best to get away. He catapulted all over the stable, he fell over, he shrieked, he even bled; but all the time the man who could clip anything clung to his head like a monkey on a stick and the clippers whirred. I couldn't bear to watch so I walked up and down outside and felt faint. I went green and white and hot and cold until the man who could clip anything limped out of the box to tell me that my horse was finished. Next time, he said, could he have the pleasure of doing the whole job, not just the ears; then perhaps the horse would realise he was not at the slaughterhouse.

The day of the opening meet arrived. Splendidly arrayed in the full hunt coat, the velvet cap, and the long, shiny boots in box calf, I mounted the chestnut with the lop ears and the three white socks and rode with Glynis to the meet. I was apprehensive but confident. During the weeks which had led up to this day I had spent many contented hours hacking my new hunter and his excellent manners had never wavered. Faced with hounds however, things were rather different.

The trouble started at the meet when Glynis and I rode up to a group of acquaintances who had hitherto been standing quietly on the hall drive. The chestnut refused to stand still; with his head tucked into his chest and his tail high, he sidled and fidgeted and set off all the other horses, so that in the end Glynis and I were forced to move on to escape all the barging. In the midst of this the hunt secretary, an impressively mounted gentleman in scarlet rode up to me and asked if I had compounded. In my anxiety to prevent my horse from energetically digging a hole in the master's drive with a front hoof, I couldn't think what he meant, but I said yes and hoped I had.

The chestnut now progressed to outright prancing and half-rears. I was in danger of losing my nerve but Glynis voiced the comforting thought that the chestnut's excitement was just a temporary lapse and he would settle down as the day went on. She asked me how the

. . . he didn't like the clippers

advertisement had been worded. Between kangaroo hops I explained about the 'six-year-old gelding, quiet and well-mannered. Hunted two seasons.'

"Of course," Glynis said thoughtfully, "hunted two seasons does not necessarily mean he is a good hunter."

She was right. With hounds in front of him the chestnut turned into a flying machine. His tremendous stride outstripped all. When I found myself amongst the thrusters of the first flight, even the bold, hearing the snorting as of a hundred dragons behind them, stood back and regarded his passing in awe. He was not a good jumper either. He flew his fences at ninety miles an hour usually managing to take at least half of them with him; the deepest plough in Hertfordshire slowed him not; the thickest bullfinch, the densest cover laced with blackthorn and bramble daunted him not.

M'am, poor m'am in her full hunt coat who only wished to tootle, spent most of the day clinging somewhere in the region of the handlebar ears, uttering occasional quacks of panic whenever she felt obliged to open her eyes.

My husband, observing our return, woman and beast liberally spread with mud, with something akin to wonder, enquired how I had enjoyed my hunting.

With a stoicism that could not have been bettered by the fitter of the khaki breeches, I replied that it had been very exciting. I extracted eight thorns from my horse including one which had completely pierced one of his lop ears. There followed a bath and some deep thought. The next day I went to the saddlers and bought a drop noseband, a standing martingale and a pair of limpet riding gloves lined with pimpled rubber and specially designed for restraining pulling horses. I wasn't going to give in without a fight.

. . . he turned into a flying machine

An Incident in Suburbia

I have to report an incident. Our hounds, flagging but tenacious, running without huntsman (whose mount had landed upon a willow stake), or whipper-in (whose horse was later discovered upended in a ditch with the unfortunate soul beneath), or field (which, led by the master, bellowing, scarlet-faced with impotent fury, were irretrievably lost some four miles distant), have entered suburbia.

There being in the path of the pack a hedge, neatly shaved to a convenient height, they lolloped over it, accidentally bowling over the housewife who was collecting parsley with which to garnish the family supper. Innocent of the enormity of their crime, they gathered around with many an apologetic lick and slurp, paused to greet the pram-bound baby (whose wonderment at the confrontation of those laughing faces, flying tongues and pensile ears can only be imagined), and gambolled away in order to run their quarry to ground under some sheds in a nearby allotment.

Realising the potential of such an event, the local newspaper enthusiastically inflated the incident to massacre proportions. Faced with eager reporters sniffing avidly at the scent, the housewife's imagination streamed away breast high. The exhausted hounds became, in a trice, a wild-eyed bloodthirsty pack. Their perfunctory greetings became, in no time at all, a preliminary to savaging the most delicate parts of her anatomy and gobbling up the baby. The photograph which accompanied this dramatic report showed the mother standing upon the parsley bed, the babe clutched defensively to her bosom. The League Against Cruel Sports, invited to comment, proclaimed, "This is just another example of the cruelty and arrogance of those who indulge in this sickening and barbaric sport."

Yesterday there was a similar incident, albeit with slightly different consequences. Your correspondent was one of a small group of followers who, besplattered and catching the breath after a brisk run, were standing outside a pair of farm cottages, when we were startled by one of the occupants who, shrieking and throwing her apron over her head, ran down the garden path towards us.

As this hysterical apparition approached, dismayed and horrified glances were exchanged by the followers, who envisaged banner headlines in nothing less, this time, than the *Sun*, the *People*, and the *News of the World*. Nevertheless, we stood our ground.

As she reached us, however, we realised that this fine show of amateur dramatics was the result of nothing more sinister than a state of great excitement.

"I saw it!" she shrieked. "It came under the palings and went straight across the grass and down the side of the leeks, and the hound was almost on him and he opened his mouth . . ." She paused for breath and opened her hands to demonstrate the gaping jaws.

"And then what?" we cried with one voice, hardly able to contain ourselves.

Her face fell. "And then he tripped," she said apologetically.

Yesterday morning I had spent two hours strapping and plaiting the flying machine, half an hour getting dressed (including repairs to the hair-net, wisping the full hunt coat, wrestling with the good linen stock), half an hour driving to the meet, a quarter of an hour trying to find a suitable place to park, a further half an hour plunging unwontedly about at a dry meet, mouthing anxious platitudes to villagers who, regardless of the danger of dancing hooves, lifted up little Johnny, the better for him to poke the horse in the eye; and finally two hours pounding from covert to blank covert, the limpet pimpled gloves locked grimly upon the reins in a vain effort to restrain the flying machine.

When, at last, hounds put up a fox, everyone was taken unawares, lighted cigarettes flew through the air, the flying machine stood on end despite the standing martingale, sandwiches were trampled underfoot. Sylvia lost the stopper from her flask; good brandy fountained into the air and fell, lost, into the grass. Faithful to the last, Glynis and I struggled to control our horses as others galloped past, but by the time we had combed the turf, drunk the remains of the brandy in case the stopper remained undiscovered (it didn't), we had missed most of the run; and the hound, in tripping up, missed the fox.

By the time hounds found again, it was impossibly, unseasonably hot. At the check, people peeled off their gloves and lifted their hats to aerate their plastered scalps. The horses steamed and dripped until the outside of the covert resembled the inside of a Turkish Bath.

When hounds picked up the line again, the field followed but with less enthusiasm than before; even the flying machine was not entirely beyond control and allowed himself to be steered through a convenient gap and round the edge of a pond with many an uneasy glance at the soupy green surface. Next there was a headland to ride and a ditch to negotiate before we hit grass and the pace became faster, the country more open. There was a surge as hooves hit the turf and the sound of thundering hooves and rasping breath in my ears; and galloping beside me, a complete stranger gave me a beam of perfect joy.

Ahead I could see hounds with all of the hunt staff strung behind them. The huntsman's little horse by Pinza was going like smoke as they swung in a wide arc and made for the lane; they were almost within snatching distance of the brush when the school bus laboured round the bend. As it ground to a halt, all assumed the driver to be a sporting countryman loath to foil the scent.

But no, arriving in the lane in a welter of clattering hooves and skidding on the tarmac, we saw that he had run over the fox. Hounds ran hither and thither under the bus, the master was suffering apoplexy, the school children hung out of the windows filled with horror and elation at the unexpected turn of events.

I couldn't help wondering, as I hauled at the head of the flying machine to prevent him conveying me into the ditch, what Nimrod would have made of such a day.

A Hunt Ball

It was all right until the lights went out. There we all were, just warming up at the hunt ball when, phut . . . nothing. No lights, no heat, the disc-jockey cut off in mid-bleat and the lead singer of the Dark Blues left mouthing into empty air.

We were all optimistic about it at first. People stayed on the dance-floor, frozen in attitudes of revelry like courtiers in Sleeping Beauty, or participants in a game of Statues. "It will be reconnected in a minute," we told each other. "It's just one of those unfortunate things, one of the small eccentricities of the Southern Electricity Board. A new man. The wrong button. Somebody's mug of Horlicks knocked over and shorting the system."

There was a bit of giggling. A few scuffles and an isolated scream. People chattered at first then, as the minutes passed and the lights didn't come back, they stopped chattering. A questioning silence filled the expensively draped marquee. It spread among the guests at the linen-covered tables, through the big house where the log fires burned in their cast-iron baskets, where the magnificent flower arrangements, made dark and hideous, squatted in the corners, lurked in the alcoves. It penetrated into the discotheque where the young people looked round by the light of a flickering candelabra and realised for the first time that they were in a chapel; it passed upstairs along galleries hung with paintings, to where a Jack Russell sat defensively outside his master's bedroom on the second landing. It made the cloakroom ladies uneasy. "We're cursed," they said. "First the loos are blocked, now the lights have gone."

A glimmer of light was greeted with a cheer that tailed off into misery as it was revealed as an emergency supply. The giant blow-heaters were blasting ice-cold air into the marquee at calf-level. Would-be dancers felt and fumbled their way back to their tables. Voices grew loud and anxious. "Is anything being *done*?"

There began a persistent rapping from one end of the marquee. It took a little time for everyone to realise that their attention was being sought. The master stood between two candelabra flanked by two hunt servants in full livery with flowers to the right and left of him. As one recently risen from a lying in state before startled mourners, he began to speak.

"I have to announce that there has been a deliberate act of sabotage. The main cable carrying the electricity supply to the hall has been cut; and as specialist equipment and knowledge would have been required, this has clearly been a planned and premeditated action. We are doing our best to reconnect but it is expected to take some time to restore our power. I very much regret that this should happen to us tonight. We are doing all we can."

The message ended, but the master's unspoken anger trembled in the atmosphere. Whisperings began, springing up here and there like wind amongst winter-dry rushes, although there was no reason to whisper. "Is it the League Against Cruel Sports?" "Could it be the IRA?" "Shall we stick it out or go to my place?" "We didn't pay twelve quid to die of pneumonia." We were shaken and offended. An occasion we had long relished had turned sour. The evening seemed lost.

Then suddenly, from the middle of the marquee somebody began to sing. He didn't sound too sober, and he might not even have noticed that the lights had gone out. People listened to the unsteady rendering, "D'ye ken John *Peel*, when he's far far *away* . . ." and they smiled again; they joined in. There was at once a change of heart. Candles were lit, glasses chinked, gentlemen fetched coats for the ladies. There was a rush to claim breakfast before the hotplates went cold. The tombola swung into action. As people flourished their knives and forks they cried that, even if one couldn't dance, well, there were other things one could do. They cast speculative eyes over the collection of bottles rapidly being distributed by courtesy of the hunt, and at other people's wives.

When the lights came back, it was almost as much of a surprise as when they had gone out. People blinked at each other in delight. A wild cheering began. The heaters blew hot air over numbed ankles. The Dark Blues made their way back across the dance floor. The young people ran for the discotheque. The master beamed. People left their tables to dance as the music began, leaving a litter of bottles and bacon rinds and discarded fur coats.

Nobody found out who had cut the cable; but it was generally agreed to be the best hunt ball for years.

Remnants of the Chase

I had just taken off my party dress when I thought I heard the Valkyries pass. It was a sound of thundering hooves, the wailing of the banshee, the baying of hounds and the howls of the dying.

When I put my head out of the window I discovered it was November the fifth as well. I could see stars, flashes of light, orange sparks and dark scuttling figures. Then suddenly the hallucination passed.

Elaine stood on the road in a long purple dress and many necklaces.

"Where are the horses?" I asked.

"Gone," she said.

After a luncheon party in aid of the wire and poultry fund at which one has consumed an unwise quantity of champagne and brandy cocktails, one needs time to ingest information like this. When it did sink in, the reaction was total panic. I pulled on my jeans first back to front, then in the conventional manner, and I told myself the horses had gone. This self-addressed information, which began in a tone of calm acceptance, became, as sobriety returned and I reached the stable yard, a babble of terror.

Elaine stood by the car clutching headcollars and a bucket half-full of pony nuts. She said, "They'll be killed. If they get to the dual carriageway, they'll all be killed. If they cause an accident people will be killed as well."

In the way that circumstances can turn one's friends into strangers overnight, I couldn't drive the car. The familiar vehicle that had pulled my trailer, had carried a spent hunter back from hunting, was as alien to me as a rocket ship.

"I can't find the starter . . . where are the lights . . . the choke . . .?" Whilst I gabbled and fretted and pressed everything, activating the wipers, the washers, the indicators, the radio, Elaine leaned her head on the bucket and whimpered on about who and what would be killed. By the time we lurched away, the dead had reached Borodino proportions.

During our oscillations along the village street and out into the lanes, we said, "They'll be grazing on the verge . . . in the football field . . . They'll be on the Bury Drive . . . in the farmyard." These wan hopes and quackings kept us going until we reached the junction, where it was no longer possible to avoid the obvious: that horses galloping alone in the darkness would pass the quiet fields and shadowy gateways, heading for the only thing they could see, the neon-lit Cambridge to London road.

As I indicated to turn onto the A10, first to the right and then to the left in a welter of indecision, two things happened. Firstly the horses passed by. They galloped out of the darkness and across our vision, necks stretched, rugs flapping, hooves ringing out on the road. They galloped resolutely, and like horses on a merry-go-round there was a steady relentlessness in their passing. Behind them, a stream of nose-to-tail traffic urged them on, illuminating their flight and hooting at them.

Bleating helplessly, we sat on the incline, waiting for the traffic to pass. I was just about to move off when one of the rear doors was wrenched open and two dark figures leapt into the back seat. My husband and Elaine's fiancée had been pursuing the horses and it was predictably them, but their abrupt arrival unnerved me. I stalled the car. As it began to slip backwards everyone shouted. Elaine upset the pony nuts, and David said, "Oh God, she'll kill us all," in a tone that suggested it might be the best way out of a nasty situation.

Home-bound traffic on the dual-carriageway would not let us pass. Frustrated drivers assumed we were a car-load of drunken revellers, to be studiously ignored if not actively thwarted. We scuttled in their wake, hooting, flashing our lights, shouting, waving buckets and displaying headcollars out of the windows to illustrate our good intent. We made abortive dives for the inside lane, the outside lane; we contemplated the gap between.

The others urged me on in desperation.

"Put your foot down and aim for the middle!"

"Go *on*, Caroline! Make them let us through!"

"I can't," I said weakly. "I just can't." The gap in the middle of the vehicles was only two feet wide.

"Switch your lights to full beam!"

"Put your hand on your horn and keep it there!"

Suddenly the traffic picked up speed.

"We're going faster," I said. "The horses must have turned off!"

"Turn back!" everyone cried, refuting it at once as I braked hard, only to be hooted at from behind: "Keep going, you fool, you'll cause an accident!"

We raced round the roundabout and back up the dual carriageway to where a wide grass verge bore the unmistakable dent of hoofprints. Other traffic had turned off before us, stalking the horses up the narrow lane. It was impossible to overtake. We fretted behind, lamenting and cursing.

Deranged with impatience, David opened the door and jumped out. He vanished from sight instantly with a horrified cry, having misjudged the speed of the vehicle. A moment later he reappeared, racing past the car like a madman. He tore off his smart blazer and hurled it into the hedge. He never saw it again. He did catch up with the horses though. He actually managed to stop them. The traffic had stopped as well and as he grabbed the nearest horse by its mane, it was mightily unfortunate that another car should hurtle round the bend at that particular moment and slam into the flying machine, bowling him over in the road.

The vet surveyed the damaged chestnut, and told me I was lucky. I didn't feel lucky. I stood holding the pail of bloody water and I tried to feel lucky, because my poor flying machine would only be out of action for three months.

Elaine looked miserable. The long purple dress was not what it was. In the sharply-lit stable we were an unedifying sight, with our tangled hair, our smudged mascara, the vet called from his fireside, the bruised and bleeding horse. The aftermath of the party. The remnants of the chase. The Requiem for a Hunting Diary.

Grey Days

On the day the new horse came the rain started. That is not to say it had not rained before. It had been, fellow subscribers never tired of informing me, the wettest season in living memory. Out with Elaine on foot one day before the advent of the new horse, we had a conversation with a gentleman who was standing in the centre of a twelve foot puddle. "Of course," he said modestly, as Elaine aimed her camera to capture for posterity the dripping horse, the water spouting from the brim of the bowler hat, "we are not at our best."

The joint master of the Enfield Chace loaded up his horse and slammed up the ramp. "The rain won't stop us," he declared. "It may stop others but it hasn't stopped us yet." He climbed into the Land Rover and drove off with the light of battle in his eye. Outside his gates, the engine petered out and caused a traffic jam that stretched back into the town centre. That's just how it is. You sally forth crying, "To hell with the weather," and the damp gets into the battery. It sours the soul. It breaks the spirit.

The new horse was grey, the colour of the dingy sky and the miserable, mud-filled horizon. People told me I was mad to buy a new horse for what was left of the season. "Will the rain ever stop?" I asked those I met in the lanes where the ditches gurgled. "No," they said.

Warm and weatherproof in the full hunt coat, I boxed to the next Wednesday meet with the new horse. People who had regarded the flying machine with consternation now appeared surprised and even a little shocked.

"What on earth have you got there?" they asked. "Where's the nice-looking chestnut horse?"

"This," I said, indicating the little, grey cob with the roman nose, the bent hind leg and the hogged mane, "is more suitable for the country."

"Webbed feet?" somebody said, in a wry tone.

"May I have your attention please?" the master boomed. He took up a position in the back yard of the Duke of Wellington and the field of twenty-five gave him their undivided attention through a chain-link fence.

"What did I tell you," Glynis whispered. "He's packing up; the farmers don't like us on the land in this weather."

"Keep well away from the pheasant-rearing pens," the master told us severely. "The last time we met here it was reported that some of the field rode amongst them and anyone who does so again will answer to me. One field sport must respect another. I thank you."

The cover behind the pheasant-rearing pens was vast and around the edge at regular intervals were little shelters constructed out of bales and corrugated iron; there was corn inside, and clean water. The rides through the cover were clean and well kept.

. . . of course, we are not at our best

"There won't be any foxes here," Glynis commented. "It's too well–keepered."

"I'm surprised they let us in," I said.

"Shooting is over now," Glynis said, "and anyway it's like the master said, one field sport must respect another; we allow them to shoot on hunt property."

The little, grey cob stood looking into the wood where hounds were working. Raindrops ran down his pricked ears. He didn't prance and sidle like the flying machine, he didn't cavort and barge into other horses.

"He certainly seems the perfect gentleman," people admitted.

When we moved on to another part of the cover he trotted along behind in an unassuming fashion, as one who knows his rightful place. He didn't fly at the ditches at ninety miles an hour, he approached them steadily and with caution, hopping over them neatly, content to wait his turn. He let others gallop past without so much as a flip of an ear and he stopped on a sixpence.

People were impressed by this display of good manners. "He is an honest, little fellow," they said. "Even if he does look as though he comes with the milk on Sundays."

Standing at the edge of a ride a goodly interval of time elapsed and people began to look at their watches. There was no noise from the cover, no whimper of hound, no sound from the horn, no cracking of twigs. Nothing.

The field master frowned. Had they moved on without giving the sign? Had they – inconceivable thought – found and streamed away in silence, without being noticed? The trees dripped steadily and the field waited on the ride, but the woods were mute.

A hound appeared first, wandering in an aimless way out of the cover to stand on the ride with its stern waving slightly. Another came. It lifted its nose and sniffed the air in a half-hearted way then sat down and began to scratch itself. More hounds appeared; then there was a commotion in the wood and the hunt servants came.

The master came first. He cantered up the ride and his face was perfectly grey. He said, "I am a sportsman and accustomed to death, but what I have seen today has made me feel sick."

We who were the field stood as if turned to stone, our hearts frozen under our sodden coats and our thoughts turned to unspeakable things; the Marquis de Sade, Glencoe, Crippen. We didn't know if we wanted to hear what the master had found in the wood, why hounds were scattered over the ride, why the master felt sick.

To the side of the field stood the foot followers and amongst them, three keepers from the estate. The master saw them and the colour returned to his cheeks. He stood in his stirrups and he thrust out his whip. His thunderous bellow probably put to flight every adult bird for thirty miles, sent every poult into a nervous moult and addled every last egg.

"FIVE DEAD FOXES HANGING ON A FENCE!"

Five dead foxes hanging on a fence. One field sport must respect another. All the hunt horses have mud fever. All the fields are plough. The full hunt coat has sprung a leak. The perfect gentleman doesn't want to go into the trailer. The car won't start.

Happy, happy days.

The Young Entry

"When do you want them?" the kennelman said.

"When do I want what?" I asked.

"The hound pups," he said.

I had forgotten I had promised to walk a couple of puppies for the hunt. "Oh," I said vaguely. "Next week?"

"I'll bring them myself," he promised.

Holding out my arms in the innocent belief that I was about to be handed two snuffling, whimpering bundles, I was unexpectedly almost flattened by a wet steamroller in the shape of two enormous, gambolling creatures, which, slubbering and gobbering in an ecstasy of Baskervillian delight, leapt out of the back of the terrier van.

"Nice, aren't they?" the kennelman said fondly. "They get on well with curs," he added, as they bounded towards the Cavalier King Charles whose eyes were starting out of her head, and the Jack Russell terrier, whose hackles were up like the backbone of a stegosaurus.

Sue, a helper who alternated between bars and stable, watched their arrival impassively. Behind her back she held a red plastic water bowl with 'Doggy' on it. Later she gave it to the tortoises. The 'pups' were given a washing up bowl. When they had chewed that up, they had an earthenware pot. After they had broken that, they had a metal bin with a slow leak. It was all not quite how we had imagined it.

The arrival of the hound puppies stirred the imagination of the village; it threw up its united arms in dismay, prophesying overturned dustbins, uprooted rose bushes, an untimely end to all its cats and the total annulment of all hope in the Best Kept Village Competition.

Sue, finding herself landed with the exercising of the puppies, enquired of hunt supporters what course this should take. Presenting a sober countenance, they informed her that the requirements were simple. She would be required to blow the correct notes on a horn for their education, to exercise them for five walking miles per day, to carry a whip and a thong with which to effect their discipline, and from time to time she should let out a hoik and holloa, being sure to wear a scarlet jersey at all times in order that they might learn to recognise and respect the colour. Feeling that all this was too much to expect from a loyal, if not at all times devoted, servant, she gave in her notice.

The problem of play, embracing the confines of the garden and paddock, was one of constant surveillance and much anxiety. A sneeze, a mere blink of an eyelid and they were missing. Valedictory faces peered over the fence. "They 'ounds is on th' green agin!"

The proximity of the churchyard was another problem; brown bones of frightening length and familiarity were quickly interred in our muck heap whilst the pups, front paws and noses black with tilth, were locked in the stables.

Offerings for their continued welfare arrived periodically from the kennels; worm tablets, a couple, a horse's leg, lovingly propped against the kitchen door. Sue sat on the back lawn cutting it up.

. . . bones of frightening length and familiarity

"I don't recognise it," she said uneasily, "but I can't help feeling it might be someone I know."

The barman passed by with a crate of empties in each hand. "If the public health come round now," he said, "how are you going to convince them you don't use it in the *Boeuf Bourguignonne*?"

Out across the stubble with a couple of hounds and a good terrier to act as anchorman, the world takes on a rosy hue, although a rabbit can reduce the size of the party to one within half a second. On the day we irretrievably lost one of the pups after a similar incident, we practised the best and most delicate way of informing the kennels that we had mislaid one of their best hounds.

A van drew up outside. We stood to attention in hopeful expectancy as the sliding door opened.

"Is this your bloody stupid dog?"

The missing person, sitting gratefully upon the passenger seat, gave the rescuer's face a gobbering, slubbering lick, leaving strands of saliva dangling from his ears.

"Eeeyuck!" the rescuer said in disgust, pushing the hound unceremoniously off the seat and driving away before we had uttered a word of thanks.

When our hounds went to join the rest of the young entry back at the kennels, Sue and I delivered them in the trailer. They stared at us in bewilderment through the little personnel door, their lowered faces creased into anxious folds, their eyes drooping with expressions strangely reminiscent of Clement Freud.

The kennelman was hacking at the ribcage of a casualty racehorse. "My!" he exclaimed when he saw them, "they've made fine big bitches. Master'll be pleased with them!"

Thrust into the exercise yard with the others, our puppies were immediately lost in a jumble of lemon and white; unbelievably, we couldn't tell which they were; unbelievably, they didn't come to the bars when we called them; and unbelievable though it seemed, it was right and proper that it should have been so.

A Perfect Gentleman

This matinal hour is not altogether in his favour. From the suspicious light in his white-fringed eyes, to the ungainly tilt of his curby hocks, this little cob pleases me not. The coat, even with the passing of a calendar month, still has the appearance of having been scraped with a safety razor, every cat-hair a-tremble and standing erect like the protection on an under-ripe gooseberry. He is not a pretty sight.

Never was a silk purse so painfully wrought, as the fingers numb and aching, prod and prink at the bristly mane in the endeavour to produce the seven round plaits and forelock. The needle pierces the finger, the calm of the stable is upset, the grooming box turns turtle. The last of the hoof oil splatters the kicking boards and the needle is irretrievably lost amongst the bedding. If ever a pastime were over-rated, then hunting is it.

What use the full hunt coat, the good linen stock, on such an aberration? Snivelling and grizzling, I unload a mile from the meet. Even the old, grey mare, pressed into service by Elaine, unclipped and fluffed out like the snow goose, has an elegant turn to the neck and a raking stride. This little cob slaps his boxy feet purposefully, bone-shakingly, upon the tarmacadam; his starched ears, nastily close to my own, straining for a sound, a clue to the whereabouts of hounds.

Outside the hostelry, mine host proffers turbid punch with reluctance; broken-veined faces are pinched with cold above alpine stocks, thoroughbred skins ripple convulsively like wind over wheat. Villagers stare with sullen satisfaction, their collars up, their hands thrust deep into their pockets. The huntsman trots by, his shoulders hunched, calling to hounds; subscribers back off, seemingly offended, irritated by the show of action.

The glass is empty and there is nothing to do but to follow, clattering along the lanes at a rate to set the bursal enlargements popping up like soda bubbles. In the wake of the field one treads the heels of a proliferation of red ribbons; the season progresses and the kicked horses turn into kicking horses out of sheer self-defence. Why have I bothered to come out today, when all the world is in such an ill humour?

Slithering to a halt on a patch of ice outside the covert, lifting gloved hands to blow hopelessly upon frozen fingers, incredibly, on this the worst of all days, hounds come tumbling out and go walloping across the plough, chiming like the Bow bells.

The miserable congregation in the lane is at once transformed into a plunging, rearing litter of horses which flies wholesale up the bank and into the plough.

"Hold hard! Hold BLOODY HARD!" the field master shouts; but most are already gone. This little cob covers the plough in a succession of rubber-ball bounds, landing in a bundle of horses in front of a ditch. With no time to waste, we push through the hedge and, scratched from ear to ear but uncaring, gallop along a headland where the little cob leaps a top hat; the owner is ahead, desperately trying to turn his horse, he can't afford another!

Now we have hit grass and the wind makes our eyes run and

Laundry Gorse looms ahead flanked by its famous, cavernous ditch. Now the smart thoroughbreds teeter on the brink of the yawning chasm, and slipping, slithering in indecision, pass the point of no return and leap wildly for the opposite bank, their riders paling the while. The old, grey mare has refused but the chestnut alongside has taken off and unaccountably dropped like a stone out of sight. Wondering faces peer over the edge to meet the anxious eyes of the rider, still in the saddle and wondering how he is to get out; there is no time to see, because hounds have swung over to the right where there is an accommodating tractor crossing. We gallop in single file along the edge of seeds, down a lane with a hideous clatter, and through a farmyard where there is a horrific twanging noise as someone gallops through an electric fence.

Now the field master has turned and is shouting a belated warning to the rest of the field.

"Mind the wire! Mind the BLOODY WIRE!" he yells in agonised tones.

Ahead are some perfectly horrible studies in horsemanship at a fallen tree which is blocking the ride. This little cob stands off and goes up like a lift, peering down from an unwarranted and unusual height to ascertain the suitability of the landing sight. Along the lane

. . . a perfect gentleman

someone is on foot, leading a limping bay; an omen, for at the same time, a hysterical pony runs backwards and gives the little cob two shod feet in the chest. Is he damaged? Is he lame? He doesn't feel it as we leap another ditch and traverse another headland, the box calf boots torn by brambles, the full hunt coat whipped by over-hanging branches; the two-way stretch breeches are a mass of pulled threads and even the Herbert Johnson receives a crack from a flying flint which removes a piece of the pile. A flint strikes the cheek of a gentleman on my left, whose agonised yell and welling blood would gladden the heart of any anti-blood-sport sympathiser.

Hounds have lost the fox but there is blood aplenty on the faces of subscribers and on the legs of their horses. Investigating the kick, I discover that the little, grey cob has been holed. He thinks nothing of it and would go on, but I find the two distinct hoofprints and the hole alarming. We ride away from the rest of the field; the old, grey mare's plumage is soaked and sodden. Above us, the first flakes of snow begin to fall.

Towards the dusk, the little, grey cob is pulling at a hay net, hung with striped blankets, his neck edged with friz. I have filled the hole with *Protocon*, plastered and pointed and smoothed the surface. I am content that there will be no lameness and little swelling; I shall be hunting again by the weekend. How, I wonder, could I have felt less than satisfied with this kindly animal, when a blow such as this delivered to the flying machine, would surely have knocked his leg off? Why, in the soft light of the stable, the creature is almost handsome. Truly, the evening is altogether in his favour.

The Sport of our Ancestors

At the meet, the girl with the long, blonde hair and the red, drainpipe jeans, standing beneath the poster promising eternal damnation to all who participate in blood sports, looks familiar. On close inspection, and to my everlasting embarrassment, it turns out to be my daughter.

Things have reached a pretty pass, I tell you, in this household. We have done our bit. In our time we have subscribed to Save the Whales, No to Nuclear Power, Stop the Seal Culling, and Keep Cruise Missiles Off our Doorstep. The other day we even received a personal missive from Billy Graham, thanking us for our support. Of course, we subscribe to all these causes only indirectly; that is, we dole out the pocket money and it ends up helping to finance Rainbow Warrior.

Do not imagine for one moment that I disapprove of all this. In my youth, I might have done the same, but nobody pricked my conscience; the lines of communication to my little acre were not so active. These days, if somebody kicks a dog in Winnipeg, the next morning they know all about it in Derby; we're all so much better informed.

It has to be said though, that this latest activity sticks in the gizzard. Our worst enemies could not deny that we are a sporting family; and that our sports, rather than being of the bat and ball variety, have been of the field, the stable and the covert. Our daughter has lived her life in the midst of all this. She has grown accustomed to her nearest and dearest staggering, hollow-eyed, downstairs in the dark of a winter morning, to mix feeds, to break the ice in the bucket, to plait manes with numbed and purple fingers, to toil and to sweat and to swear and to hitch up trailers in the noble cause of hunting. At the meet she has been dandled on many a pommel and has been encouraged to fondle the noses of hunters, hounds, and even horses. She has been known to run over the fields dragging a rabbit (the unfortunate victim of a fatal road accident) on a string, in order to test the nose of the hound puppies walked for the kennels. And there was never the slightest indication that any of this was against her nature.

But these children of ours have been schooled to face a suspect world. They have been taught never to take things at face value, but to probe and pull apart, to examine and question, to discover the hidden truth, the deeper motive. They are capable of reasoned decision. ("Thank you for the series of articles," the assistant editor of *Pony* magazine once wrote. "We like them very much. However, I doubt if we will use the one on hunting, as many of our readers disapprove of it.") If they refuse to accept things on the slender grounds that their ancestors have advocated them since time out of memory, we can hardly gnash our teeth. We shall have to swallow hard and accept that our traditions will be slipped under the microscope; that hunting, together with the class system, public schools, marriage, the monarchy, meat-eating and the traditional Sunday lunch, are up for re-appraisal.

"I always return home better pleased with but an indifferent chase, with death at the end of it, than with the best chase possible, if it end with the loss of the fox." So wrote Peter Beckford. Yet speaking as a follower, I have to admit that the part I like least about hunting, is catching the fox; and that digging out a fox who has provided a good run seems to lack essential sportsmanship. On the other side of the coin I am aware that hunts are in business to kill foxes, and if they fail, farmers and land-owners will no longer welcome hounds on their property; not to mention the five hundred mounted followers churning along behind.

Of course, very few people actually go hunting with the express intention of killing a fox; apart from the hunt servants, most of the followers do their level best to make sure that hounds never get near one.

At the meet, anyone with half an eye can see that the followers encourage their horses to kick, jump and stamp on hounds in order to reduce drastically the size of the pack. At the covertside, they holloa away everything – blackbirds, rats, cats, game-keepers, and, in moments of extreme desperation, fieldmice and voles – in order to confuse and exhaust the remaining hounds as quickly as possible by keeping them flying from holloa to holloa. Should hounds actually manage to get away onto the line of a fox, the followers waste no time in crowding them by galloping close on their sterns, over-riding them whenever possible, and crossing and re-crossing the line at every opportunity in order to foil the scent.

Car-followers also do their bit by clogging the lanes with their vehicles, leaving their engines running and their chokes out, thus causing a smog in which to misdirect the hunt staff, who are forced to traverse the lines by riding the ditch bottoms.

The fact that most hunt followers are on the side of the fox is, of course, a well guarded secret. Only on the day of retribution, when eternal damnation is nigh, will it all be allowed to spill out. We shall reveal to the wondrous host that the only people who really wanted to catch a fox were the ones with the brass buttons and the long floppy ears. It may prove to be our salvation.

Of Bogs and Fogs . . .

Resplendent in the full hunt coat (refurbished to twice its former glory by Moss Bros.' valet service), encased in gleaming box calf exactly to the knee, helmeted by Herbert Johnson himself, I contemplated with mouth agape and eyes rounded with stupefaction a wondrous creature, lately risen from the uliginous bog, sullage a-tremble on every limb, snorting like a paludial dragon, pounding the paddock to a pulp, splattering the fruits of its wallowing upon the good linen stock fastened with the real gold pin, a gift from one of the best people.

Glynis, arriving with a grinding of gears, hauling up the handbrake in the manner of a Bombay taxi-driver, rounded the corner of the stable block in order to enquire as to my readiness for the meet. She opened her mouth, but the words stuck in her throat.

As the apparition galloped by the rails yet again, reins and stirrups flying, the saddle so recently burnished with Stübben saddle-soap now caked, no, spread, with unctuous Hertfordshire mud, I said (and with admirable restraint under the circumstances), "Do you have a gun? I would like to shoot it."

Indeed, this has not been a carefree season. Only days before the escape of the immaculate hunter, there was the morning of the fog. Traffic inched uneasily along the lanes in an interminable procession which caused us to miss the meet.

Whilst unloading the horses in some unknown and desolate spot, the impenetrable mist swallowed us in an instant. Glynis said (her

. . . a wondrous creature, lately risen from the bog

voice coming from an unexpected quarter and making me jump), "Will we find them?"

Feeling the air in order to ascertain that I was indeed mounted, the little cob being grey and exceedingly difficult to distinguish in a mist, taking a firm grip on my rubber-covered reins with my limpet gloves, and coiling the thong of my hunting whip (which is spoiled by an unfortunate plastic handle, owing, Moss Bros. unflinchingly informed me, to the scarcity of good quality bone), I cried reassuringly that surely we should locate them, having the advantage of four pairs of eyes to see with, eight ears to hear with (four of them with independent suspension), twelve legs with which to cover the country; not to mention my flask filled to the brim with Remy Martin. How could we fail?

Two hours later, fumbling along a damp and disembodied hedgebottom, we came upon a couple of hounds. Canine, equine and representatives of *homo sapiens* peered at each other with ill-founded exultation. After which, jointly perceiving that the country about them remained as silent as the grave, each face fell. We halted a while in each other's company, the fog around us growing thicker, the air becoming colder, our world bereft of hunt and horn, our hearts bereft of hope. Suddenly, one hound, finding it all too much to bear, sat down, lifted its eyes to where the sky should have been, and began to howl. The little, grey cob, by no means an imaginative animal, gave an involuntary shudder which vibrated through my Harry Hall two-way-stretch breeches, via the two pairs of tights for added insulation, to my blue and frozen thighs.

"That," Glynis said with feeling, "is just about how *I* feel."

Of course there was a morning when one awoke to a sky of virgin Basildon Bond, when the sun on the distant winter wheat turned the fields to Harrods' green and the leaves in the stable yard crunched underfoot like giant cornflakes. The day began to sour when Albert flew backwards out of the Belvoir Supreme trailer, for reasons never wholly comprehended, searing Glynis' ungloved hands on the halter rope, scattering farm labourers like chaff on the wind, clipping the Mercedes smartly in his passing (leaving a small scar on the diaphanous paintwork), and a legacy of half a shoe on the ramp as confirmation of his non-participation in the sporting life. This was seen as the ultimate defeat for the subscribers, who, not entirely thwarted, grabbed stable-companion Victoria, albeit unwashed and unplaited, and missed the stirrup cup again.

Our local turkey farmers organised a shoot and bagged six foxes in an afternoon, displaying a polaroid photograph as indisputable evidence for the hunt, who had previously discredited the idea that there were foxes in the vicinity. In the interests of good relations, they organised a meet with only a passing reluctance, due to the preponderance of anti-hunt investment landowners and the proximity of the main London to Cambridge road.

Reynard Vulpine took off in all directions from the first draw, between the legs of foot followers, and under the noses of astonished hunters who had not had a good look at a fox in five seasons. Typically, hounds picked up the line of one who, knowing what he was about, ran like greased lightening into forbidden territory. The farm manager, who had been lying in wait for such an affront, arose from the bushes in a villainous fury; and in uncompromising language, before many hushed and uncomfortable sportsmen, blasted the hunt to hell and worse.

With fine dignity the master said, "I have hunted this land the whole of my life, as did my father before me, and his father before that. I am not going to be thrown off by a mere farm manager." Replacing his goblet of port on the bar of The Sword in Hand (where this splended oration had taken place), he turned to the terrier-man who, quivering and twitching with apprehension, had been standing at his elbow, and added serenely, "Now go and tell him."

To Finish the Season

End of season dispersal sale of one undersized, rather common, hunter gelding. Unreliable in traffic, capricious to catch, dislikes clippers, has been known to kick other horses. On the bonus side, schooled at Benenden, jumps anything, goes first or last.

The proud new owners are already on their way to collect their purchase; and leaning over the stable door, I stare at the advertised, who in turn, spooklike in the darkened stable swept clear of bedding against his departure, stares back at me. Can he know as, terrier-like, he cocks his head and regards me with eyes, large, black and anxious, that this is the parting of the ways? Did he realise, as his tail was washed, his hooves scrubbed, his mane neatly laid with egg white saved from breakfast, that this was the very last time? Probably not. Since the unintelligent beast has no way of knowing that hunting has finished, he is probably waiting to be transported to the meet.

The last day was not a success. It began on an unpromising note with a squalid little scene at breakfast-time. Elaine's stock and gloves had somehow been bundled into the washing machine with the red bistro tablecloths. There was, at the critical moment, a yelp of dismay, followed by an unfair accusation, which grew, word by heated word, into a pitched battle, whilst the toast burned to a cinder and the eggs boiled dry. Finally the injured party howled that the defaced garments should be compensated for by the owner of the washing machine. It was all too much to take. I was stung to retort that such a claim was rendered null and void by the fact that the stock was one of mine anyway; and the gloves, to my certain knowledge, belonged to Glynis. We took our separate paths to the meet.

Eleven o'clock on the village green on this last of days. Already the sun is up, dispelling the slight frost and any hope of scent. The hunt servants are down to their last three horses, and unsinged cat hairs wave gently in the breeze.

Glynis, on foot (Albert having developed a curb, Victoria a cough), and waving Elaine's camera for the purpose of souvenir photographs, clicks the shutter experimentally and darts hither and thither, recording the arrival of hounds, and the arrival (separately) of Elaine and me. Misgivings previously voiced, on her enthusiasm for the subject over-riding her scant knowledge of the mechanics of photography, proved justified even before hounds moved off. From our separate ends of the green, the injured party and I observe with wonder our souvenir photographer, her person garlanded with exposed black film, still bravely snapping well-mounted followers and hunt servants, who, flattered by the attention, but baffled by the ringlets of celluloid curling from every pocket and clearly emerging from the camera, smile hesitantly.

The lanes we traverse at a rib-rattling, sweat-inducing trot smell of tar and petrol. Scales Park, where we drift aimlessly for several hours, smells of spring and warm earth, and sap.

Hounds move contentedly through the plantations, unhurried, pausing for a stretch or a scratch. Horses reach for twigs unrebuked and their mouths drip brown and green froth. Followers fall to discussing their summer holidays. The sun is too warm on one's heavily-coated back; the catkins are golden. The air is filled with the sweet breath of horse and the pungency of pine; but the gloves and the stock are undeniably pink, and the hunting is a mere formality.

There is a mild dissatisfaction in riding home (in single file – Elaine and I are acquainted now, but not yet familiar) with the box calf still gleaming, the breeches unsplattered, and the little cob as dry and white as a newly-laundered sheet. There is none of the perverse satisfaction felt on reaching the stable after a day battered by winds, stung by sleet and drenched by icy rain; only a feeling of mild irritation that the season should peter out on such an insipid note.

. . . thinking he is going to the meet

Now there are changes ahead; for this is the end of the Hunting Diary and goodbye to hounds and to the little, grey cob. There are to be no souvenir photographs. To Glynis' complete bewilderment the film turns out to be blank. After much soul-searching, the camera was proclaimed to be faulty; that or the chemist who bungled the developing of the film, which after all, may have been a dud anyway.

The approach of a vehicle proclaims the arrival of the proud new owners. The vendor, who is regretful, yet determined to be totally without sentiment, flies into an immediate panic as the little, grey cob walks obediently up the ramp into the trailer. Will they take care of him, these unknown people, whose thick wad of notes I hold in my sweating palm? In his old age, when his Benenden schooling and his jumping ability have faded, leaving the other, more enduring qualities of unlovely conformation and querulousness in their wake, will they allow him to grow white and whiskered in the landscape, or will they ship him on the hoof to the Continental butchers?

"And by the way," I cry after them as they slam up the ramp, "if you *should* decide to part with him again, you will let me know. . .?"

But the anxious voice of the previous owner, who is now full of regret and whose eyes suddenly overflow with sentiment, is lost in the roar of exhaust and the rattle of alloy as the trailer moves out of the yard, carrying away the little, grey cob who probably thinks he is going to the meet.